Badge #1 – Memoirs of a Boston Cop

The incredible account

of the career of

Frank M. DeSario

by Frank M. DeSario

Edited by Shelly Rosenberg
www.ShellyRosenberg.com

Badge #1 – Memoirs of a Boston Cop

Badge #1 – Memoirs of a Boston Cop

Contents

Forward

My husband Frank M. DeSario has performed many heroic acts during his career as a police officer in Boston. One incident of which I am extremely proud occurred in 1987 when he saved the life of a young baby. I personally wanted to share this with you, the readers of his book. Below find the report of commendation from the Police Department of Boston.

Geri De Sario

Boston Police   August 10, 1987
Recommendation for Commendation
Francis M. DeSario - Police Officer – 6063
Special Operation

Describe the incident and commendable actions taken:

On Thursday, June 18, 1987, Officer Francis M. DeSario, while off duty was in the harness shop of the Hughes Horse & Rider Supplies, 151 Randolph St. Canton, MA.

While inside the shop, Officer DeSario heard what sounded like a muffled thump, then a great deal of commotion followed by hysterical screaming coming from outside the rear of the building. Officer DeSario, along with several other people, rushed outside to find that the ten (10) month old grandson of the store's owner had fallen down a flight of fifteen (15) stairs, striking his head on the cement landing. The baby had been knocked unconscious and had stopped breathing. As the family members and other store customers froze in shock and could not help, Officer DeSario immediately rushed to the aid of the infant. Not knowing the extent or seriousness of the baby's injuries, Officer DeSario gently and carefully began CPR and mouth to mouth resuscitation. About one and a half minutes later the baby began to breath. Still not knowing the extent of the baby's injuries, Officer DeSario gently resisted the families efforts to take the baby and managed to keep the infant immobile until the ambulance arrived to transport the child to the Goddard Hospital where it was treated, held and diagnosed to have suffered a fractured skull.

The doctors at Goddard Hospital along with the Canton Fire Department Ambulance EMTs Rick Russell and Al Duty, both stated that had it not been for Officer DeSario's immediate capable and caring assistance given to this child they would have certainly lost the baby.

Officer DeSario, the humble and unassuming professional Officer that he is, returned to work the following night, never mentioning the incident to his fellow police officers and only after receiving an emotional and grateful letter from the baby's grandfather were we made aware of and able to investigate this incident.

Officer DeSario is to be commended for his quick response, his calm and professional handling of an emotional situation and his humble exit from an incident that had he not been present would have certainly resulted in the loss of a helpless baby. This Officer is a credit to himself, the Special Operations Division and the Boston Police Department. I therefore strongly recommend that he receive departmental recognition and commendation for his professional action while off duty.

Sgt. Kevin D. Foley, I.D. #6827

Badge #1 – Memoirs of a Boston Cop

A transcript from the Boston Police Journal, Fall 2002, states the following:

Francis M. DeSario, police officer of District A-1, now has the distinguished honor of being the longest serving officer with the Police Department. He was sworn in as a Boston police officer on March 11, 1964. He now has 38 years and more than 8 months as a police officer. The #1 badge was passed down to him by retired fellow district A-1 police officer Jack Bilodeau, who served 39 years, 3 months, and 22 days. Enjoy your retirement Jack. Francis M. DeSario was appointed to the Boston Police Department on March 11, 1964. He began his career working in the Tactical Patrol Force for almost 10 years. He has had further assignments in the transportation unit, area-B, and finally in district A-1 in 1991 where he will finish his career. Along the way, he has received numerous awards and commendations for meritorious service.

Frank received a commendation in 1977 after he observed a motorcyclist who had crashed into a guard rail and was quickly covered in flames from the leaking fuel tank. Frank attempted to pull the man to safety but was unsuccessful because the cyclist was trapped. Frank then ran to his car, grabbed a blanket and attempted to cover the man. Once the blanket caught fire, Frank took his own jacket to put out the fire. More EMS personnel arrived and rushed the man to the hospital where he survived. As they took the man to the ambulance Frank was heard saying, "I only wish I could have done more for the poor guy."

Frank finally wears the #1 badge as our district A-1 motorcycle officer assigned to a downtown crossing and the North End. Keep up the good work Frank.

1

Beginning of the Ride

I'm finally sitting in front of my computer trying to work up enough courage to do something that I've wanted to do since my retirement in June of 2003. I had completed thirty-nine years and three months on police service with the Boston Police Department. Now as I sit back thinking about my career I can't help thinking about how much I want to share my experiences with others.

Thinking way back, I remember wondering what I was going to do with my life. Here I was, nineteen years old, without a care in the world, living at home with Mom, Dad, and two kid sisters. My big brother Mike (my idol) had just gotten married after being discharged from the U.S. Marines. Mike urged me to go to civil service school and try to land a job with the local police department. At the time, I was driving a truck, making a few bucks, and had a beautiful blonde girlfriend named Geri, who I had been dating for two years.

When Mike spoke, I listened! So off I went to enroll in Matt Connolly's Civil Service School. The course lasted for about six months. After I completed the course I took the test and passed. I was put on a list and told to wait.

The year was 1961 and Geri was also thinking about her future. She was hoping for an engagement ring and to set the special date. That year, things were acting up in Southeast Asia and the Selective Service was starting up the draft. I joined the U.S. Army Reserves and began my six months of active duty and six and a half years in the Reserves. I was discharged in February 1962, came home, and found that my girl had made our wedding arrangements for April of 1963. We got married on April 21, 1963.

So, it was back to work for me, driving a truck while wondering if the police department had forgotten about me. It turned out that they had not forgotten about me. On March 11, 1964, I began what would be the most exciting and sometimes the most unrewarding job a person could have.

2

How Proud I Was

Wow, could this be for real? Me, a pretty tough kid from the Roxbury, Dorchester area of Boston realizing that staying out of trouble as a kid is really going to pay off. I must not forget to mention, the training that I received at St. Patrick's Grammar School by the Sisters of Charity (Halifax). I cannot forget also the training at Holy Cross Cathedral High School in the 'South End' of Boston. And finally I cannot forget the most important influences in my past, the iron fists of my dad and my Marine brother (Mike) guided by the boss of bosses (my mom).

So here I go, thinking I'm big and bad and could handle anything!

Wednesday, March 11, 1964, a day this recruit will never forget.

It was a cold, gloomy day. I was sworn in, at 10:00a.m., by Deputy Superintendent Taylor at Boston Police Headquarters on Berkley Street. I was addressed and welcomed by Commissioner Edmund McNamara and then later was assigned to the training unit of the Boston Police Academy at 7 Warren Avenue. I was still wondering if all this was really happening.

I'll never forget being issued a winter uniform coat, and a hat with badge #1315. We were later greeted by Deputy Superintendent Cadigan at 1:00p.m. We were then issued our lecture materials and other equipment by Lieutenant Burke, and then finally I was addressed by Sergeant Barney Schroeder regarding the Academy rules. (COULD THIS REALLY BE HAPPENING?) The one thing I'll never forget is how proud I was.

3

Reality

The activities at the Academy were mostly routine, learning about the evolution of the Boston Police Department and also the critical areas of the department.

March 18, 1964

It was a cold, snowy day. We received our revolvers which were Colts 38s. Now the boring stuff began to decline and the good stuff was on the way. On that day, we began by learning the proper use and care of our revolvers. My class consisted of forty-five young, eager men who could hardly wait to hit the street. I remember, up to this point, we had received only one pair of pants. This was specifically curious to me because it was winter. The time in the academy seemed to drag by but it was apparent that this training was essential in order to be a good officer. Okay, three weeks at the range and now you're ready to hit the street with a veteran. This was on-the-job training but we were still attached to the Police Academy.

Okay guys, reality sets in!

Badge #1 – Memoirs of a Boston Cop

Monday night. May 10, 1964

Alone and away from my class, there I was, wearing a pair of winter pants, a new starched shirt, my shiny new badge which I had just received (#1315), my Colt Revolver and my six inch service baton. I was walking into station #10 at Roxbury Crossing, which is one of the toughest precincts in the city, to begin my first tour of duty in a cruiser. Oh, how I'll always remember, 11:45p.m. roll call, standing and hearing my name called along with veteran Officer John Carozza, and the look on his face as if he were saying, "Oh shit, why me?." Getting into the cruiser, I remember him saying, "Hey kid, we're the 10A car. Get in and don't touch the radio."

So far everything was routine but just around midnight Carozza spotted a car on Hammond Street. In those days, the siren was located on the roof of the cruiser connected to a small button on the dashboard. Not knowing that you were supposed to hit the button intermittently, I held it down as we were chasing the stolen car through the streets of Roxbury, causing the siren to burn itself out, creating the awful smell of burning wire. Meanwhile, two people in the "hotbox" jumped out and ran in opposite directions. I chased my suspect into an alley which was surrounded by tenement houses. There I spotted him standing next to a dumpster and holding a knife. "This can't be. It was my first night on the job." As I pulled out my service revolver, the suspect bolted into the night. At that exact moment, my partner appeared and screamed at me. "PUT AWAY YOUR GUN, IT'S ONLY A STOLEN CAR," he said, not seeing the knife. Oh, how I'll never forget going back to the station, my mouth as dry as the Sahara desert, with sweat pouring down my face. But that was not as bad as the things that John had to say about 'his being with a rookie who pulled out a gun on a stolen car suspect and not putting him with a rookie again.' I felt like the loneliest cop in the world...WELCOME TO THE REAL WORLD!

Graduation Class from the Police Academy
Frank DeSario is in the front row, sixth from the left.

4

Blood and Guts

May 12, 1964, Weather: fair and cool

Back to station #2 at Milk Street... While the class is waiting for our next set of assignments, we all talk about our experiences on the street through the city. While I thought my tour of duty was the worst that could happen, it appeared that one of the things that we learned was that nobody wanted to work with a rookie, especially the older veterans. What most of us agreed was that the old timers felt that we were cutting into their territory and had interrupted their routine. I guess we all had our horror stories to tell and we all agreed to do our best and work for them to accept us. THIS IS THE WAY IT WAS FOR YEARS. All rookies were treated this way. As we went upstairs, we held our breaths because we were about to get our new assignments. As it turned out, I had a great assignment walking on Commonwealth Avenue tagging cars.

May 15, 1964, Weather: rainy

Boy how things changed on this job! At this point I was in the North End, a walking beat on Richmond to North Streets where I remained until June

Badge #1 – Memoirs of a Boston Cop

11, 1964, all as part of on-the-job training. Everything was going well, an occasional drunk arrest, traffic arguments; everything that I could handle. I was getting (I guess you could say) a little cocky, or as they say in the Navy 'a little salty.' Then, just as I was getting used to what I was doing, at 8:45a.m., while I was tagging on Prince Street, I observed two men fighting. Both of them were going at it at a good clip. One of the men, a guy by the name of 'Red' Scalafanti, turned on me unexpectedly with his broom handle, and struck me on the top of my head. That resulted in a profusion of blood that was dripping down my face and onto my white shirt. I remember looking up at him like he was a Roman Gladiator. Well, I was in good shape too, and I'm sure he later wished he had never met me. While all of this was going on, somebody put in a call that a rookie cop was in trouble in North Square and he was bleeding. Cars and wagons were coming from every direction. All three of us were taken to the hospital where I was treated for a laceration of the scalp and scraped knuckles. Later, 'Red' Scalafanti was arrested and booked at District #1 for assault and battery with a dangerous weapon. Okay, so now what? What do I do? Where do I go?

Like I said, WELCOME TO THE REAL WORLD.

Badge #1 – Memoirs of a Boston Cop

Tuesday, June 2, 1964, Weather: fair

Ordered to appear in municipal court for alleged assault!

You know, walking the corridors of a court house for the first time as a police officer ready to testify, not knowing where you're going or whom I was to see is an awful, lonely feeling. Then, I was approached by a gentleman who said he worked in the court. He then proceeded to tell me how Mr. Scalafanti lost his temper with this other gentleman, and that he had never intended to hurt me. He then, somehow, persuaded me not to seek complaints against him, stating that he was a community worker, and he made him apologize to me. I was so relieved about not going into the courtroom, and knowing that Scalafanti would always remember me.

The sad part of my first arrest was something I found out later. The gentleman of the court was a Boston detective named Frank Mirabito, whom I encountered a year later. We had a conversation and needless to say it was unfriendly. How could another cop, especially a detective, not help a rookie cop by not aggressively pursuing a complaint and a felony conviction? Remember that we were still assigned to the Academy. We were recalled on June 22, 1964. We were all waiting for Graduation Day on July 10, 1964 from the Boston Police Department on Legion Highway.

Badge #1 – Memoirs of a Boston Cop

My First Permanent Assignment

It was only a few days out of the academy. I felt that I'd earned my right to be there, wherever I was...District 13 Jamaica Plain. Where's that? Something I'd learned in those short months, unlike being a civilian, is to always be alert and always think. Now I could relate to St. Patrick's Grammar School, remembering that every classroom you entered had a sign above the door, which read THINK.

5

First Assignment

What more could a guy want? I married the girl of my dreams, had a good job paying $108. weekly, and we were expecting our first baby in October. Back then when you worked the night shift you worked beginning at 4p.m. Working Jamaica Plain was sometimes boring as it was not considered a busy 'house.' But you never knew. The one good experience I had occurred on July 20, 1964, when I was assigned to work with a guy named 'Red' Walsh for a morning watch.

'Red' was a former Marine, who somehow got to fight in IWO JIMA at age seventeen. This guy had more guts than anyone I had ever met. Most of the time, during the morning watch, the cars would 'dig in,' but not Red, he was always looking for the bad guys, as was the case on that morning at 3:05a.m. (A 'dugout' is a favorite place an officer will go if there is nothing going on in the street. An officer might say, "I think I will dig in for a while," and go to his favorite spot.) Red spotted a Chevy convertible whose occupant was wanted for indecent assault and battery and a supermarket hold-up in Jamaica Plain. I remember three of the men hiding in the car behind the supermarket, and Red reaching in and grabbing one of the occupants whose nickname was 'Kid Boston' who was wanted for indecent assault and battery and maiming (biting the nipple of a breast off a young girl). The other two men ran in the direction of the grounds of a Catholic Convent. Red and I went in, checking the grounds of the unlit area. All at once, as if by total instinct, Red aimed his flashlight at the corner of the field while drawing his service revolver. All of a sudden he noticed there was a man crouched down with a gun pointed in our direction. I think I froze, but Red jumped on him, taking the gun away from him. All this occurred with no other cars available. What a cop, I thought!

Things started to heat up in Boston, the Vietnam War was escalating, and with that, the protests began. Students started marching in protest, crowds were out of control, and the city had to do something to keep the peace.

Enter Tactical Patrol Force

In 1962 under the direction of Commissioner Edmund McNamara, the TACTICAL PATROL FORCE was created. It initially consisted of a few detectives and a handful of men under the leadership of Captain John Hanlon the first Commander of the TPF As time went by it was obvious that the size of the unit had to be increased. In July of 1964 Headquarters started recruiting new members into the Tactical unit.

On Wednesday, July 29th I was interviewed by Deputy Superintendent Howland to be a member of the TPF On Monday August 3, 1964 I reported to the Police Academy to begin duty with the Tactical Patrol Force. From that first day on August 3rd to August 15th we received extensive training in special weapons, shotguns, pistols and riot control formations. We watched numerous films on riot control and physical exercise taught by Officer Jon Dorr of the Boston Police Department and State Police Lieutenant Owens.

Upon completion of our training the Tactical Unit was used in many ways. When we started we had no more than three cruisers. This unit on foot saturated the city's hotspots walking two abreast from the combat zone to Codman Square in Dorchester. We also worked at times as decoys dressed as old ladies or homeless people and sometimes drove taxis trying to root out those who committed serious crimes. And yet we were utilized at a moment's notice for crowd control.

I can remember vividly walking the Park Square area one night and then being picked up by a bus along with other members of the TPF. While in the bus, we were informed that there was big trouble in the Harvard Square area and that it had been overrun. When we arrived and the bus doors opened the troops could not believe what was going on. The town was literally being burned to the ground. Upon exiting the bus and falling into riot formation Lieutenant Bill McDonald, "Mr. TPF" gave the order to "move them out."

The Tactical Patrol Force did its thing. We were able to clear the area so that the Fire Department could enter Harvard Square in which there were many small fires. There we were, forty Tactical Officers "McNamara's creation" wearing our new jumpsuits, black boots and helmets and armed with our new three-foot batons. Looking at this group one could see that it was made up of mostly ex service men all in the six foot tall range. I remember the ride down there and how we were singing "God Bless America" as the bus was coming to a stop and how the bus was being pelted with bricks. On the bus with us with the hopes of giving us spiritual help, was one of the bravest Catholic priests I have ever met. His name was Father Jim Lane, Chaplain of the Boston Police Department. Getting off the bus I can remember more than one man offering Friar Lane his service baton which he promptly refused.

Well you guessed it; the first to get hurt "slightly" was Friar Jim. Before going into action that day I can remember trying to get into the proper riot formation and not being able to do so because of the debris being thrown at us. Eventually the rioting stopped and partial peace was restored. After returning and getting into the bus we were met by the town manager a Mr. Sullivan. He proceeded to walk the aisle of the bus scratching his head, then stopping to say thank you and "God Bless the TPF. Without you we would have lost Harvard Square." We returned to Boston and then on to TPF headquarters where I remember having what they called a critique session. Later, the following week Headquarters started getting mail condemning the tactics of the Boston Police Department and inquiring as to who are the TPF? Word quickly spread about how fast and disciplined we were and how we were being requested to patrol other parts of the city. It was such an honor being a member and wearing the TACTICAL PATROL FORCE patch on our upper right arms. The unit had gained so much respect because of our actions in Cambridge.

We were there for riots in Roxbury, anti-war protests, and in South Boston in 1974 to protect the children both black and white because of the start of forced bussing. Again and again we were called in and we always did an outstanding job. Many books were written about the TPF and how necessary and aggressive we were. Finally sometime in 1978 some so called community leaders in the Roxbury-Dorchester area determined that yes, the TPF was too aggressive in their tactics. Sadly, with pressure mounting on City Hall, it was goodbye to the TACTICAL PATROL FORCE.

Sitting back in my recliner and reading my diary from the early days of the TPF, I remember working with my partner, Gerry Meehan, and because we worked so well together we were picked to work undercover in the Vice Control Unit. Our main objective was to be observant while looking for booking activity, prostitution, and to field interrogation reports on suspicious persons in the North Station area.

That assignment began on February 25th on a cold, windy day. I can remember sitting in bars such as Landmark Cafe, The Four Winds, and Mario's Deli. Gerry and I would sit at the bar sipping on a beer - always draught - since the department was paying for it. Some of the time we looked grubby and in most cases we were "made." (Being made refers to working under cover. Sometimes in disguise and in hostile territory, someone in the crowd spots you and knows you are a "cop," thus the term "he made me.")

If nothing else, we shook them up as their

operation slowed down for a while. The bookies knew the TPF undercover men who were in the area. We continued that assignment until March 6th, spending on the average $4.00 a day. Neither Gerry nor I was a good drinker. I remember at the end of the week after working the North End and walking into Lieutenant Paul Russell's office hoping to get reimbursed with probably $20.00 and how we tried to look completely sober. But Lieutenant Russell always gave us that look that made us feel guilty. Without a doubt Lieutenant Paul Russell, later to become Superintendent Russell, was probably the smartest boss I had ever worked for. He had the ability to look into one's eyes and tell if he was being lied to.

Gerry and I were then chosen to go undercover driving taxis. There had been a rash of holdups in the city, and the pressure mounted for more protection for the cabbies. We came close several times but we missed getting our prey. And then, one night after driving around for hours with Gerry by my side, we 'dug in' in a secluded area in the Washington Park section of Roxbury, the high crime area of Boston. What a mistake that turned out to be. Before we knew it, we were surrounded by at least ten Boston cruisers, our brothers, all with their guns drawn and proceeding to drag us out of the cab and throwing us to the ground while we kept yelling "we're cops, we're cops." Let me tell you something. We learned a lesson. It was no fun looking down the barrels of so many revolvers.

We also had teams decoyed as street people hoping to nab those who were mugging people in the downtown area. We worked in teams of three with one officer acting as if he were drunk with his wallet being noticeable from his right rear pocket. The idea was that if the mugger spotted him and tried to rob him, the other two officers would move in and make an arrest. If the robbery was taking place, the "victim" would drop a white handkerchief to alert the team.

Most of the time it was boring with an occasional arrest but there was one night I'll never forget. We set up our team in front of the old Hillbilly ranch in the Park Square area and this night I was to be the "drunk." Things had been slow and I guess my team wasn't alert. I acted the part, my wallet sticking out as I leaned against the "Ranch," when all of a sudden a mugger approached me wielding a knife while attempting to take my wallet. I managed to drop my white "hanky" knowing that my team would move in. Well it seems my team was distracted and did not see that I was being robbed. While struggling with the suspect, I managed to get to my service revolver and arrest the mugger. Needless to say I was furious. No one got hurt and from time to time we still talked about it. What a night!

You can believe that after that experience we had a meeting and all agreed to never let our guard down when working that operation. All in all we were very successful in that we made several good arrests.

Gerry and I were on a roll. When not working undercover we would be together in a cruiser either in the combat zone or in Roxbury making some good arrests. At times we felt like bounty hunters due to the fact that we were given two days off for every felony arrest and one for any misdemeanor arrest. I remember Gerry and me playing the Magnolia Street area, a dumping ground for stolen cars, and an area very familiar to me, having grown up and playing as a kid in the area. Well in a very short time Gerry and I accumulated over twenty-eight days. As a team, Gerry and I worked well.

<u>Badge #1 – Memoirs of a Boston Cop</u>

TPF on patrol in the Combat Zone

Frank DeSario is driving and

Gerry Meehan is in the passenger seat

Frank DeSario right and his partner Gerry Meehan

apprehend a suspect for breaking and entering

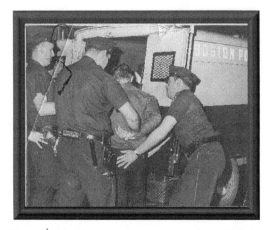

TPF officers making an arrest in the Combat Zone

Frank DeSario is on the far right

Officers Frank DeSario far left,

Ken Hegner center and

Gerry Meehan

at TPF headquarters

6

Flexibility

Okay, so now I've been on the street for a couple of years, what next? Next comes the most thrilling, the most exciting, and also the most dangerous time of my career.

June 6, 1966 (D-Day)

At this time I was detailed (assigned) to the District Attorney's office, Homicide Squad. How proud I was! Here I was, not quite twenty-seven years old and working with the detectives of detectives.

Things were heating up in the turf war for control of illegal activities in Boston. The turf war was on in Charlestown, Somerville, and Roxbury. Bodies were popping up all over the city. Connie Hughes from Charlestown, Buddy McLean from Somerville gunned down on Broadway in his hometown and rumors that more were in the planning. The Bennett Brothers from Dorchester were missing. District Attorney Garrett Byrne was very concerned, so concerned that he created a Task Force whose sole duty was to investigate Gangland murders and to put a stop to them.

Garrett Byrne selected a veteran investigator,

Badge #1 – Memoirs of a Boston Cop

Lieutenant Salvatore Ingenere, one mean sucker, who was afraid of no one. As a patrolman, he walked the streets of Roxbury, and later the Fields Corner section of Dorchester. Old Sal went up the ladder fast and was promoted to Sergeant Detective early in his career, and needless to say he knew his stuff.

On the street Lieutenant Sal had lots of contacts. Up until this point in his career Sal knew how to operate. Now Sal knew every bookie, loan shark, and good thief in the Roxbury-Dorchester area. In fact they were the source of his information. Those maggots knew that if Sal didn't get what he wanted they were in serious trouble, so he had quite a pipeline. I would often call him "Eliot Ness" because of the way he picked his men. He trusted no one yet he had to pick a squad. He began by recruiting Detective Joe McCain and Detective Leo Papille from the M.D.C. (Metropolitan District Commission) Police. Then he took his old friend from his days in Dorchester, Arthur Cardarelli, from Boston. He got John Enright, Donald McGowan and a cop from the North End recruited out of the TPF, "Injun Joe" Conforti, one tough sucker and former lightweight contender, and me the runt of the litter.

I met Sal when I was a teenager and he had the Fields Corner walking beat. My old stomping grounds were the Lucky Strike Bowling Alleys where I liked to play the pinball machines, especially the ones that paid off. One night I had a lot of money invested in the machine when in walked Officer Ingenere. He walked over to me and said for me to "screw." I told him I would, in a minute, as I had a couple of dollars invested. Well Sal grabbed me by my shoulder and threw me out the door. As I got older and wiser I learned to keep my mouth shut and to be nice to the law especially Officer Sal and especially because I worked in the Fields Corner section. Slowly we became friends, so when I joined the Boston Police he remembered me. And because I had a good record with the TPF, he recruited me.

So here we were comparing ourselves to Eliot Ness and his gang and how confident we were that we would be successful. REMEMBER I AM WRITING THIS IN 2004! Looking back to those days we were pretty much aware of the goings on throughout the city. What we did not know back then was the goings on in South Boston. Oh we knew Whitey Bulger and how he was the kingpin of all illegal activity in that area. We also knew that he was friendly with many law enforcement officers and he was considered by some to be a sort of Robin Hood in Southie. We also knew of his relationship with Stephen Flemmi. We knew they controlled the   gambling   and   loan   sharking operations in the Dorchester area and how they paid tribute to the North End. What we didn't know was that these scumbags were being protected by the F.B.I., the State Police and yes even to the Boston Police.

These maggots were allowed to do whatever they pleased. I can remember locating a garage in Roxbury where cars belonging to hit men were being stored including a gold Oldsmobile owned by Joe Barboza. I remember how I thought I had hit the lottery. Then as I was leaving the garage, I was met by a Boston detective who asked me what I had. He stated he was from Intelligence and would I mind not reporting what I had found. I agreed. The next day those cars were gone.

Now looking back I consider myself lucky for getting out of that outfit in less than two years. Here we were the DA's task force, out every night looking and waiting for suspects; only to find out they had been tipped off. I remember our office getting a call that a Joseph "Chico" D'Amico was about to be clipped. This guy was a close ally of Joe Barboza. We knew where to find "Chico." He would be in Squires, in Revere. Lt. Ingenere along with detectives Cardarelli, Leo Papille and I jumped into our unmarked 1964 stick-shift cruiser and headed out to Revere Mass. We pulled into the parking lot of "Squires," a swinging joint on the outskirts of Boston. Lt. Ingenere ordered Cardarelli and me to enter the establishment and see if "Chico" was sitting at his usual table at the end of the bar. I remember walking in with Cardarelli, my heart pumping a mile a minute and being patted down more than twice on the way to D'Amico's table.

I knew Chico because of his many appearances in municipal court. He always felt easy talking to me. Chico was far from being an angel and had many arrests and convictions for assault and battery with a dangerous weapon and he was very good with a knife. So there I was sitting at his table accompanied by Guy Frizzi, and one James "Jimmy" Kearns, two notorious hit men. I relayed the message to Chico that he may be in trouble concerning his life. I then told him that Lt. Ingenere was in the parking lot and wanted to talk to him and that he could help him. During this conversation, my legs were shaking so much I couldn't control them. With the conversation coming to an end, Chico asked us if we wanted a drink which I gladly accepted. Arthur already had one. Now Chico stood up, thanked us and said he knew about the contract but to tell Sal thanks anyway. I said goodbye to Chico, gulped down my "VO and water" and started to leave. Kearns and Frizzi gave us hateful looks.

Badge #1 – Memoirs of a Boston Cop

Out to the parking lot we went to tell Sal what had just taken place. He told us to stay in our car and to be ready to roll. The next few minutes I just sat behind the steering wheel nervous and hoping not to fuck up. Shortly thereafter, Chico, along with Kearns, left the club and entered a green sedan with Kearns getting behind the steering wheel and taking off at a high rate of speed onto Route 1 toward Boston.

At that very moment across the highway, in a parking lot, a black sedan proceeded to follow the green sedan with Kearns driving and Chico in the passenger seat. Now here we were in our 1964 stick shift Ford, trying to keep up a pace close to Chico which was impossible. They exited the ramp, where we observed Chico's car wrapped around a tree, steam coming from the engine. Sal jumped out and ran to the driver's side to get Kearns out while I opened the passenger side door and had Chico fall into the street, his forehead blown off.

Kearns was standing outside the car with a smile on his face. This infuriated Sal. All of a sudden Sal ordered his men to arrest Kearns. Now there stood Kearns bleeding slightly from his left cheekbone where it was later determined he had been grazed by a bullet. Kearns then yelled to Lt. Sal "what am I being arrested for?" Ingenere replied, "Accessory before and after" and then said to Kearns, "You set Chico up." Not only was Kearns shocked, but so were his men. The reason for the hit, we found out later, was that Chico tried to enter a downtown club owned by a Mafia member and was denied entrance. With that Chico proceeded to call the owner a "motherfucker" which turned out to be the end of the story for Chico D'Amico.

Mug Shot of Guy Frizzi, hoodlum
and associate of Joe Barboza

Badge #1 – Memoirs of a Boston Cop

Mug Shot of Arthur "Tash" Bratsos

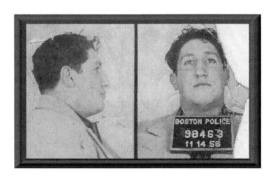

Mug Shot of Vincent "The Pig" DeVincent

7

Joseph "The Animal" Barboza

The hit on Chico infuriated Barboza (Joe the Animal) originally from the Fall River-New Bedford area where he once was a professional boxer and then worked as a leg breaker and enforcer for the local mafia guys. Joe got a little ambitious when he saw the cash flowing in and realized that he was getting only a small slice of the pie. So now Joe, after being a very efficient hit man for the local guys, decided to move in. Before the hit on his faithful companion "Chico," he along with Chico, walked into the "Peppermint Lounge" on Stuart Street in Boston which was owned and operated by one Peter Fiumara a soldier in the local mafia. Barboza approached Peter and stated to him that he was his new partner. Fiumara, recognizing Barboza, told him to "get the fuck out." With that, Chico proceeded to cut Peter's throat from ear to ear. Later, members of the task force visited Fiumara at the hospital and after hours of questioning, Peter failed to name his assailant. Word spread quickly and naturally the "word" was a $50,000 dollar contract put on Joe Barboza. Barboza continued on his murderous ways with several bodies popping up in the greater Boston area.

Meanwhile in the South Boston -Dorchester area

it was business as usual. Maggots were allowed to do anything they wanted including murder and loan-sharking. Now remember all this was taking place in the mid-sixties. The task force was becoming increasingly frustrated. To add to that frustration, I remember working day and night trying to pick up members of Barboza's gang for questioning on murders relating to the Bennett Brothers along with the murder of a local ex-professional boxer, Tony Veranis whose body was found in the Blue Hills section of Milton, Mass riddled with gun shot wounds.

Ironically, on March 1st 1967, I, along with task force members Detectives Joe McCain and Tom Arria, left our court house office to get a bite to eat. Less than a block from the courthouse and at the foot of the hill we could hear police communications coming from a traffic jam in front of us. While investigating, we observed in one car, stuck in the traffic with a police receiver blaring, the three men we were looking for. The car they were sitting in was reported stolen, and sitting behind the steering wheel was none other than Jimmy Kearns himself, who had just been cleared of any complicity in the Chico D'Amico hit on Squire Road on Dec 8th.

We were also aware that Kearns "right to

operate" had been suspended. Also in the car was William Kelly of South Boston, Raymond Stillings and Robert Conlin both of Roxbury. All we could figure out was that as we were trying to keep tabs on them, they were doing the same with us. I remember getting a search warrant from Chief Justice Elija Adlow and then literally tearing the car apart and finding a ring with 150 master automobile keys, a baseball bat, 2 tire wrenches, a pinch bar, a set of registration plates, a pocket knife, a switch blade, several wallets, a spent 45 caliber shell, and a police transistor radio capable of picking up Boston Police, MDC, and State Police frequencies. They were arrested and charged with possession of burglarious tools, a switch blade, and larceny of an automobile. These hoods all worked for the Bennett Brothers and were close to Barboza and Stevie Flemmi.

So on and on it went - how do we get Barboza? Remember we had no idea about the FBI connection. But Lt. Ingenere was no fool; he had always been a book worm and knew the law regarding the right of arrest. Suddenly we had a warrant for Joe Barboza's arrest. The charge was "being a habitual criminal." Okay so now we can get Joe off the street, at least for a while, and let him know we are alive and well. The next morning at 9a.m. as I walked into my office, I was surprised to see the Lieutenant already in along with others from the task force plus two other detectives from homicide, Detectives Cunningham and Nee, two of Boston's best. There they were loading their revolvers, checking their ammo, loading a shot gun and preparing to go out and get Joe Barboza. It was not much of a charge but with Barboza's temper no one was taking chances.

As they were planning their strategy and putting their guns in their holsters, Sal said to me, "stay here and answer the phone." Well with that I felt betrayed, especially after all the nights I drove and got dizzy out of my mind looking for Joe. Here I was sitting alone in the Task Force office killing time by going through files of past Boston murders while waiting for the phone to ring to see how my heroes were doing when all of a sudden, while sitting at my desk behind a milk stained panel, I could hear my door opening.

Then, a moment I will never forget as long as I live happened. Sitting on my rollaway chair, I glided toward the door to see who had entered. Here I am the youngest and the most inexperienced member of the task force being met by one Al Farrese who introduced himself as an attorney. With him and standing behind him he introduced me to his client, Joe Barboza.

Badge #1 – Memoirs of a Boston Cop

Farrese stated to me that he had heard there was a warrant out on his client and Barboza wanted to turn himself in. As I looked up I came face to face with the ugliest, scariest, individual I had ever seen. (Later on in life I came down with a disease called colitis; now I know how I got it!)

Farrese stated that he wanted his client arrested and booked. The best detectives in the city were out looking for this ferocious killer. They were well armed. And here I was sitting behind a typewriter with a small five shot banker's special by my side. Luckily we had booking sheets in our desks. So here I was booking Joe Barboza. I remember asking Farrese if his client knew his Miranda rights, as if I was going to question him.

Not being a wizard at the typewriter, and proceeding much too slowly for the "Animal," I heard a grunt come out of his mouth. With that I explained to Farrese that I was going to have to handcuff his client. (This is when my colitis kicked in.) Finally finished we went into the prisoners' elevator for the ride down to City Prison where Barboza was searched and put into a cell.

Back upstairs I went, into my office, wiping the sweat off my brow and wondering what had just happened. Had I done the right thing? Should I have called for assistance? These things were going through my mind. Was the lieutenant going to be angry because I didn't attempt to call him? After thinking about what had happened, I was sure I had to book him immediately.

After a while the task force returned, looking frustrated and tired. They walked by me as I was trying to get someone's attention. Finally I caught up to the Boss and I started mumbling about how I got the "Animal" downstairs in the city lockup. He looked at me in amazement and said "are you kidding?" He looked at me as if I was crazy while we were riding down the elevator to the cell block. Sal asked the sergeant at the desk for the booking sheet and proceeded to see if it was indeed Joe Barboza. Finally a smile came to the Boss's face as he ripped up the booking sheet stating I had made a few mistakes "which I did." But what I couldn't figure out was why, in the blank provided for 'arresting officer,' the name was now Lieutenant Sal Ingenere. Well I was young and smart!

One thing I'll never forget was while Barboza was leaving after being bailed out by his attorney, Sal noticed something in Barboza hand. It was a pad of paper with the names of the officers on the task force.....

After all that, one of my tasks was to pick up the boss every morning and drive him to our office. One morning, on the way to our office Sal said to me, "Go to headquarters and sign out for a shotgun and ammo." Later I asked him "why the shotgun?" He stated that he had concern for the safety of his men and for himself. Every morning I would have the shotgun with me while picking up the Boss. And in the evening I would walk him to his door with the gun in hand. I would then leave to go to my third floor apartment in Dorchester that I shared with my wife and three beautiful kids. One day upon arriving home I remember how the gun got jammed as I tried to unload it. Not wanting to take any chances with it going off accidentally in my house, I called my big brother Mike, the former Marine. He came up to my house and we took a ride to the firing range which was no more than two miles from my house. There we fired it and checked it out.

Meanwhile, there were gang related "hits" in the Boston Area and it seemed that every time we got a good lead on the whereabouts of someone they would be tipped off and then the Lieutenant would be more and more concerned. He kept telling us to be alert.

Mug Shot of Joseph Chico D'Amico

Joe "Injun Joe" Conforti on left and Frank DeSario after searching stolen car driven by Jimmy Kearns

8

Stay Away From My House

One morning as I was about to leave my third floor apartment to go pick up the Boss, my wife asked me to wait a few minutes. She wanted to go to the store for something. Upon her arrival home I noticed a frightened look on her face. I asked her what was wrong. She took me to the window and pointed outside at the white Lincoln parked in front of our house. She then stated that as she walked by the car she noticed that the driver seemed to be familiar to her, and she stated that she thought I had his mug shot in my folder. I told her not to worry and that I was going to talk to the man in the car. Down the stairs I went trying to conceal the shotgun under my "trench coat" while walking toward my unmarked car which was parked in front of the Lincoln. As I was about to pass the Lincoln, the man behind the wheel called "Frankie get in da car!" Acting surprised, I recognize him as being the one we wanted to talk to concerning the D'Amico murder.

We had nothing on this guy, but we knew he was very capable of committing murder. I can see his face now as he stared straight ahead. I was sitting next to him with my shotgun partially exposed enough for him to see. He started off by saying what a beautiful blond wife I had and asked how many kids I had. This thug had been in many bars and nightclubs we "task forced" (visited), and although we were there, we had never talked. We had received information that yes indeed this guy hit "Chico" but had no evidence. With that, I turned and thanked him while he was getting a bird's eye view of my shotgun. All of a sudden his voice toned down; he looked at me and asked "Why are you looking for me?" I explained that our boss wanted to talk to him. And I asked why he never showed up for his father's wake and funeral. With that I advised him to go to the DA's office to explain things to Lt. Ingenere. He agreed. As I was exiting his car, I told him he would be making a big mistake if he ever showed up in front of my house again. I'm sure he got the message.

As time went on it became more and more frustrating trying to find out what was going on. The secrecy of the two squads on the sixth floor was getting to us. Here we were specifically assigned to 'gangland' murders only and across the hall top notched detectives were assigned to what was painted on their door, "Domestic Affairs." Supposedly they investigated all serious crimes *except* gangland murders. Yet when there was a hit there they were. Why? We never knew! Maybe it was pure dedication but why were we told not to talk to the men across the hall in domestic affairs? I was much too inexperienced to know the answer then. It seemed we would be out all day and night visiting bars and nightclubs and hangouts throughout Suffolk County (Revere and Swampscott) where we knew Barboza once lived, near the home of his buddy Chico D'Amico and around East Boston and the bars along Bennington Street. So they knew we were out there making fools out of ourselves while wasting gas. And here we were thinking we were doing a great job.

Looking back and knowing what we now know, it seems they had more protection than we had. And it took me over thirty years to find this out. Also looking back and knowing how much protection they had from prosecution I wonder what would the FBI do if one of us got killed? They knew we were being harassed while working our asses off to nail those maggots. Not only was it a losing game we were not making any money. But we thought being "detectives of detectives" was good enough. As I started thinking about leaving, I found out that other men were feeling the same way. Things started to fall apart from within. We all started complaining or we showed our frustration by arguing among ourselves.

Such was the case one night when the Boss

called for me to pick him up. We were going "cruising!" Well, I had just lost my grandmother and I explained to him that I didn't feel like going out. With that he raised his voice at me and hung up the phone. The next day he called me into his office and started to lay into me for not going out. I told him how I felt and that my family came first. With that he yelled at me and called me a "punk." Instinctively I lunged putting him against the wall.

Now remember please, we did not know then what we now know and yet we were always suspicious. Barboza and company knew who they had on their side. We didn't. Meanwhile the wise guys were having meetings right under our noses at locations right there in the North End. Attending these meetings were law enforcement people, friends of "Whitey Bulger and Stevie Flemmi." How comfortable Bulger (and company) must have felt having that much high ranking law in his pocket. But in the back of his mind knowing how much he knew, I can only think ... what fools they really were!

Lt. Ingenere, looking for more help, called upon two top notched detectives, Dennis Casey and Arthur Linsky to help in our endeavor to get Joe Barboza permanently off the street. Joe remembered that "habitual criminal" rap and he had always said it was a form of harassment. Casey and Linsky had information of their own, information they kept picking up from their stoolies from their days in Vice and Narcotics. They received information that the "Animal" was about to make another "hit" somewhere near a bar in the downtown Boston area on an ex con who was singing to the FBI. Joe's car was spotted on Washington Street near Congress Street when it was stopped by Casey and Linsky. Barboza knew of their reputation and how aggressive they were. A search of Barboza's car turned up an M-1 rifle with a loaded clip inside, plus several rounds of ammo, along with other weapons.

Finally we had Barboza behind bars on a decent rap. At his arraignment his bail was set at over $125,000 cash. That made a lot of us happy. Who would dare come forward and post that kind of money for a guy that hot while being hated by the local mafia guys?

Apparently the "Animal" did have at least two more friends, one Thomas DiPriscio an ex-boxer from the Roslindale section of Boston who at one time was an enforcer for local loan sharks, and another fool wanna-be Arthur "Tash" Bratsos. They admired Barboza and someday wanted to be just like him. These two men vowed to the "Animal" that they would find the money to bail him out. What a mistake. Apparently they were not remembering that their hero was a hated man in the North End. Foolishly these two men proceeded to go into a local lounge, "The Nite Lite" in the North End owned and operated by the Mafia. Once inside they told the local hoods that they were raising money for their buddy, Joe Barboza, and that they were $85,000 short.

This infuriated the patrons of the club, especially Ralph "Ralphie Chong" LaMattina, a soldier in the local Mafia. That these two friends of the "Animal" would go into the Nite Lite was unbelievable. After they stated what they were doing there, word had it that "Chong" jumped to his feet while drawing an automatic. He started spraying the two friends of the "Animal" with bullets while yelling all kinds of obscenities. Behind the bar there was a small hallway with a door leading to a very narrow alley leading to Commercial Street where there was a 1964 grey Cadillac Sedan registered to Arthur Bratsos at Doone Street in Medford, whose residence was ironically across the street from one of the Angiullo brothers. Somehow the patrons, along with LaMattina, managed to get the bodies out and into the back seat of the sedan. The next morning, November 15th 1966, a cruiser patrolling the "A" Street area of South Boston, was flagged down by a citizen who claimed there were two men sleeping in the back seat of a Cadillac. Well, there they were, one on top of the other on the floor in the rear of Bratso's car.

Word quickly spread throughout the North End about what had happened. The North End was crawling with cops. The men of the task force along with Lt. Ingenere entered the club where the rugs had been removed and the mirrors shattered. No one was coming forward with any information. To our surprise there was "commander" John Doyle and his men supposedly to "assist in the investigation." Still the North End was so hot it completely shut down the normal daily routine of booking and loan-sharking. LaMattina was out of favor with his own people.

Ralphie had to be punished in some small way. So now Ralphie willingly turned himself in and appeared before Judge Tauro along with his attorney Jimmy " Little Flower" Morrelli. With this, the Judge asked Morrelli to enter a plea to which Morrelli answered "Not Guilty," while at the same time LaMattina answered "Guilty." Morrelli, looking at LaMattina in amazement, was nudged by LaMattina to be quiet. This was their punishment for exerting so much heat which caused them to lose lots of money. So off to jail went Ralphie for being an accessory to murder. Meanwhile back in prison, Barboza was singing like a bird about the operation in the North End while trying to make a deal. It worked for the "Animal." He gave the Feds what they wanted and the Feds gave Joe what he wanted - a license to go out and kill again (which he did).

Again, now thinking back as a young cop I wouldn't let myself believe that these deals could be made especially when the information Barboza gave the Feds was all lies. With the help of the FBI this sent innocent people to jail while he was set free. I can only imagine how loud he laughed when he walked out of the courtroom.

Again let me say that was then this is now - 2005

As a young cop, I can remember thinking "well okay" at least he's giving us something and we are getting rid of him in Boston. Back then, to be honest, I had a fear of Barboza, a sort of natural fear you have when you play this game with a ruthless killer. What this did for me was make me a better cop and taught me not to be naïve. I'll admit it made me very nervous especially when he had the task force names on him. I often now think how lucky we must have been that no one in our squad ever got hurt. Looking back I realize how much Barboza must have hated us. He always claimed that the Task Force was harassing him.

The last straw.

Once in the middle of the night, my daughter Patty, who was just over three years old, couldn't sleep. I remember her walking into my bedroom as my wife and I slept. As she stood over the foot of my bed trying to awaken us, I can remember distinctively going for my service revolver (which I kept under the bed) and aiming it at my daughter. That was it, what was I doing? Working day and night, not making any money, being threatened, and working knowing something just "ain't" right. It was a daily routine for the Lieutenant to say "don't trust him" or "don't tell the detectives across the hall anything," and if you did talk to one of them and he saw you he would ask "What did you tell him?"

Finally after having some heated words with the boss, I told him I wanted out. I was sick of him telling me who I could or could not talk to, and I especially didn't like being called a "punk" even though I knew he didn't mean it.

As it turned out, the old Lieutenant was right; there were people up there that I should not have trusted.

The following month, I remember knocking on Mr. Garrett Byrne's door and asking if I could speak to him. The name "Garrett Byrne" was renowned throughout the state, especially in Suffolk County. Anyone would be proud to work for him. He looked up and said "what's the matter Frankie?" I began to mumble like a fool not knowing what he knew. As it turned out there was not much that Mr. Byrne didn't know. He knew about the friction going on on the other side of the hall and I guess he may have had a hint of what we now know. I proceeded to tell him that maybe I was a little too young to be a detective of detectives, and then I told him I couldn't comprehend all of what was going on, and maybe I needed more street experience. He said he understood perfectly and that I could come back anytime I wished. He wished me luck and asked if I wanted to go back to my beloved TPF. I said "yes" and he shook my hand.

Oh what a relief!

Off I went, into the sunset (Oh what a relief). Walking out, I felt like someone had taken a load off my back.

Thinking back I remember when I was driving a truck, having a ball, getting appointed to the Boston Police, and then graduating from the Academy. I remember being assigned to Division 13, working the 13-a car with "Red Walsh." Also I remember the night we caught "Kid Boston" and the night he saved my ass in the nun's courtyard. And I think of growing with the police department and finally being part of TPF with a bunch of guys I could depend upon. And then I think of my education with the DA's office.

By this point I hadn't received my five-year stripe and yet I felt I had already had a career.

My return to the TPF.

July 7th 1967. Captain Bradley commanding. Oh what a relief being away from the DA's office and back with the real men of the TPF. After a brief welcome by the captain it was back to the patrol car (at least for now) and back with Gerry. At first we chatted for a while and tried to get used to each other again. Gerry stated that things had been going smoothly for him and nothing really exciting had happened, and with a smile he stated "not even a dead body." Gerry was a smart street kid from the "Bronx" so when I started talking to him about the DA's office he knew what I was talking about. Gerry never wanted to be a detective. He knew that the temptation was there and if he saw something he didn't like, he'd probably lose his temper.

Here he was, ex-tank commander and former

member of the 82nd airborne being dropped by me every Saturday night so he could go to mass at his church. He used to tell me to sit and say a few Hail Marys and to not answer a call without him. One Saturday night I got even with Gerry. I answered a disturbance call and ended up getting punched in the face and I needed medical attention. The PS "Patrol Supervisor" asked me where my partner was. I told him Gerry was in church. Boy was Gerry "in the shit." When Gerry asked me why I said that, I told him that was better than saying you were in a gin mill. Welcome back to the TPF.

The Tactical Unit had the responsibility of guarding dignitaries. On July 30th, a Sunday, Vice President Humphrey was escorted by the TPF to the Sheraton Boston for a Democratic dinner. He was the first of the many celebrities I would eventually escort. That year Shirley MacLaine came to Boston for her debut in "Sweet Charity." Her agent called Headquarters and asked for two TPF men to assist her during her stay at the Sheraton Plaza Hotel. It was a snowy cold week and the agent requested to have one man inside and one man outside. Officer Al Osso, the eldest, asked me if he could be inside because he was a fan of Shirley's. I said "sure Al, I'll be outside."

Badge #1 – Memoirs of a Boston Cop

Well what happened next was bizarre. Miss MacLaine exited the hotel through the side door with hopes of doing some shopping. As she was attempting to cross the street she had to climb a snow bank which she promptly got stuck in. Observing this, I immediately ran to her aid. She held out her arms as I climbed the snow bank and proceeded to help her down. As this was happening, an alert photographer took a picture of us descending the snow bank. Appearing on the front page of the old Record American newspaper was the photo of us holding hands with the caption reading "Gallant Boston Police Officer Frank DeSario aids Shirley MacLaine out of snow bank." The next night I escorted her to the theater for her grand opening. She wrote down my name, gave me a hug and said goodbye after the show.

A few years had gone by and then one afternoon while in my kitchen watching the "Good Morning Show," a Miss Joyce Kilhawick introduced her guest for the day, Miss Shirley MacLaine. I poked my wife and told her that I know her. Miss Kilhawick while introducing Shirley McLean asked, "Have you ever been in Boston before?" With that, with my wife and kids watching, she said, "The last time I was in Boston I was greeted by a handsome Boston Policeman and I believe his name was Frank." With that they took a commercial break. Then all of a sudden the phone rang and my wife answered. "Hello this is Joyce Kilhawick from the "Today" show. Is there an Officer DeSario there?" With that Miss MacLaine got on the phone and asked me how I'd been. Meanwhile as I was breaking into a cold sweat looking at my family she started telling the audience how wonderful and charming I was, and how I saved her from the snow bank, and that there would be two tickets at the box office in the Wang Center for me and a guest. She blew me a kiss and said, "See you later."

The next night, sure enough at the box office there were two tickets waiting for me for her performance in "That's Entertainment." Here we were, my wife and I, being escorted to the front row in the Wang Center waiting for the opening of "That's Entertainment."

Then, Shirley entered the stage wearing a female version tuxedo as she began her song and dance routine. At the end of her first dance number she paused for a sip of water while her audience gave her a standing ovation. After a short pause she started to tell the audience how much she loved Boston. With that she began to talk about her last experience while in

Badge #1 – Memoirs of a Boston Cop

Boston and how a Boston Officer pulled her out of a snow bank. Then she introduced me and invited me onto the stage where upon she began to serenade me. After I turned three shades of red and there was a loud applause, she invited my wife and me backstage after the show. After meeting and talking with her backstage we thanked her for an outstanding night and told her much we enjoyed her show. Our visit ended with my wife asking Shirley, "Did you have anything to do with my husband?" I was thinking she would obviously say no, but she said "I'll never tell," but as she said it there was a large wink for my wife. Now how could this duty compare to being on the murderous streets of Dorchester and Roxbury - while receiving the same salary?

Okay, it was time to go back to work and to try to get Shirley out of my mind. The streets of Boston are different at night. It always seemed that the darker it got the more unfriendly the citizens would be. It seemed that all the good people would go indoors before dark. This is when the TPF would start their shift. The Tactical Patrol Force, the elite group of Boston Police Officers, less than 100 of them, were freed of routine patrol so that they could aggressively go after the most serious crimes. This was our world. The best part of being in this unit was that we had the freedom to go from one district to another depending upon where the action was. The high visibility created by the TPF I'm sure deterred crimes that could have happened.

The reputation that our unit had built up had spread and the word was out. "Watch out for the TPF." We also volunteered to work undercover dressing in many disguises in order to get close to the criminal element. The TPF also gave me the opportunity to visit the haunts of the crime bosses I had investigated while in the DA's office. The bad guys, it seemed, had no fear of an approaching squad car even as it pulled in front of their establishments. But let an unmarked car come close, and then they would disappear. In a way I was lucky having learned so much (probably too much) while in homicide where the officers of the districts had their own priorities, taking care of their assigned sectors. I found that it takes quite a while for patrol officers to really know the goings on throughout the city. In the short time I spent in the DA's office I learned more than what a patrol officer would learn in a career...simply because I had the resources and the availability of the upper echelon. That's why I think it's imperative for police officers to always be alert. It seemed as though everywhere I would go with the TPF every block had a story to tell.

Badge #1 – Memoirs of a Boston Cop

Working day and night in the DA's office and saturating the Roxbury Dudley Street area as well as South Boston, I was well aware of the likes of Stevie "the Rifleman Flemmi" and his cohorts as well as Bulger's crew in South Boston and the goings on in the North End. And all the while they were thinking they were on their own without any help, especially from the FBI. It just seemed that no matter how hard I tried to forget how frustrated I was something would always pop up.

Then there was one night I'll never forget. It was Wednesday the first week of October, 1968. While patrolling Roxbury, and looking at the house I was brought up in, I was in a daze thinking of all the good times and all the good people I enjoyed as a youth.

Then I received a call from my brother "Mike" and with a grazed voice he proceeded to tell me that our dad, a Roxbury oil dealer, had been lured into an apartment after delivering fuel oil at the corner of Blue Hill Avenue and Alaska Street where he was slugged, stomped and robbed of $585.00 at gun point. After being assured that my father would be all right physically, I remember racing down to District #9 on Dudley Street to talk to the investigating officers. A short time, later my brother the former Marine arrived and we both read the police report. It seemed this maggot pulled a gun on my dad and lured him into an apartment on Blue Hill Avenue. He then ordered my dad to beg for his life while putting a gun in his mouth. He then pistol whipped him and took his money and fled.

My brother Mike became so enraged that it took two of us to hold him from storming out of the station and doing something on his own. Luckily we calmed him down and convinced him to ride with us to visit the scene.

My fellow officers learned of the incident and offered their free time to help investigate. My friends had plenty of leads, but an arrest was never made. This was lucky for him because he didn't get to meet my brother Mike.

Word spread through that community that a TPF officer's father was stomped and beaten and robbed, and many of them voiced their concern. Dad, in his day, would have showed that maggot where to put that gun. But Dad wasn't a young man anymore. The irony of the story was that my dad would often give the oil away to the needy in that area.

Badge #1 – Memoirs of a Boston Cop

My father recovered but I'm sure that incident forced him to retire. One thing was clear. Roxbury, my hometown, was a place where, while as a kid, no one locked their doors. My, how times have changed!

The TPF worked the area of Roxbury and Dorchester for a couple of more years and I enjoyed it. It gave me the opportunity to watch the house where my dad was robbed.

Mug Shot of Joe Barboza

Shirley MacLaine
being helped over a snow bank
at the Sheraton Plaza by Frank DeSario

9
Utilize the TPF

The tactical unit was so unique; it was trained to perform any function that the department had in mind. We could be called to fill in at any district that was short in manpower. Vice and Narcotics would borrow some of our men to act as decoys and work undercover for drug buys. We worked the whole city, whereas the districts had to maintain their manpower numbers to keep their areas safe. There was always a bit of jealousy between the TPF men and the District men, maybe because they knew we were hand picked and were part of the Mounted Patrol, Harbor Patrol and later the Motorcycle Unit. It was truly a young man's job and man were these guys dedicated!

..................All I wanted to do was share with you some of the exciting things that have happened in my career.

I remember always wondering if I would ever have to use my service revolver while hoping that if I did, I would be justified.

It happened at 12:30am on March 21, 1969. My partner Gerry Meehan and I were on a walking beat in the Combat Zone area where just about anything could happen. This was an area loaded with pimp's, junkies and motorcycle gangs. It was a place where the meaning of "THINK" should be on everyone's mind.

Then it happened, while in the vicinity of Beach and Washington Streets as we were walking, a white male came running toward Gerry and me and was yelling "help help he's got a gun." My partner and I cautiously ran up LaGrange Street where sure enough in the middle of the street there was a man holding a gun and aiming it in our direction. He then yelled "Don't come any closer or I will kill you." He repeated that statement two more times while running toward us and firing his gun. I was running for cover behind a parked car. I remember being so nervous that while attempting to draw my service revolver it fell to the ground. I guess I didn't want to take my eyes off him. As he stood no more than fifteen or twenty feet from me, I yelled for him to drop his gun. With that he fired his gun in our direction.

Like a bolt of lightning, my partner Gerry pushed two unknown white males out of the line of fire. Gerry then yelled for him to drop his gun. Again the suspect yelled "Don't come any closer" as he slowly walked in my direction with his gun pointed at me. I knew as he was getting closer that I was going to have to shoot.

Badge #1 – Memoirs of a Boston Cop

Slowly taking aim and putting my revolver in single action mode, I kept thinking "Am I right?" Then my gun seemed to explode. Looking up I saw him still standing with his gun still in his hand, and me thinking "Could I be such a lousy shot?" All of a sudden he dropped to the ground, gun still in his hand and then I watched as Officer Dominic Fontana ran to the suspect and took the gun out of his hand. It was a loaded eight shot automatic. I remember hearing sirens blaring from all directions and I kept hoping that I had done the right thing. All I could think about while taking aim was, I was actually going to shoot a man.

Out of the darkness I was approached by Sgt. Detective Feeney who proceeded to console me. He stated that he observed the shooting and that I was justified in shooting back. Going back into the station and after being interviewed and finishing my report, I remember Gerry, Dominic, and I hugging each other for a job well done. Then, a police officer, whom I will not name, approached Sgt. Feeney while asking him to sign an overtime slip saying he was there and he assisted. Then something happened that I will never forget. Feeney yelled "Yeah you were there hiding behind a parked car and I'm considering putting you in for cowardice." Wow, we thought we didn't know whether to laugh or not. Charles "Chipper" Roy was taken to the Boston City Hospital where he was treated for gunshot wounds of the lower abdomen. The last time I saw him he had more tubes coming out of him than you could imagine.

Okay so now what? I had my first shooting out of the way, what next? I reminded Gerry of the first year on the street and how we kept looking for our first dead body call. "What would it be like?" Finally later that summer Gerry and I got a call to investigate a possible suicide at the Mass Transit Authority rapid transit station at Dover and Washington Streets. Off we went, two big tough TPF men going to a simple call. Upon arrival, up the stairs we went to the tracks, down about fifty yards. There was the body of a woman on the third rail. Okay Gerry, take a deep breath and let's be professional. There we were, it was obvious that the woman was dead. After the proper authorities had left it was our job to get the woman off the third rail. The only problem was that she was stuck to the third rail. Trying to get a three hundred and fifty pound woman off the tracks was no easy task. We finally got the police wagon and gently got her in it.

Back then it was our duty to transport victims, and so we were off to the Boston City Hospital, where she was officially pronounced dead on arrival. So now it was time to go to the morgue. I had never been there before so I didn't know what to expect. Gerry was so white I thought he was going to faint. I backed into the receiving ramp to deliver the body. Opening the wagon door, I jumped in to make sure the sheet we put over her was secure. Now Gerry was outside holding the "litter" which is head first toward Gerry, while I was in the back moving toward Gerry. Then, I stepped on the sheet keeping it from going forward with the body. Gerry was nose to nose with the body practically kissing her while putting the body on a gurney and rolling it to the receiving door, where we rang the bell. To our surprise, there stood an intern dressed in white wearing tong shoes and eating a tuna sandwich. The next thing I remember was seeing Gerry outside throwing his guts out while I, upon seeing this, proceed to do the same. Then we had to go back to the station to make out the report for the family and make a copy for us.

Okay Gerry, You got your dead body. Now shut up!

I remember going home that night feeling the worst I'd felt in years. I couldn't sleep much so I got up early in the morning to have coffee with my wife. Sitting at the breakfast table my wife said "By the way you got a phone call this morning." So I asked who it was and she replied that it was Mary Brown who by the way was the name of the victim taken off the third rail. I said to her, "What the hell are you talking about?" My wife then said that she, Mary Brown, had called to tell me that it was all a mistake. My "brilliant" wife had found my report on my desk and decided to have some fun with it.

Things were going great. It was almost the end of 1969. I had a steady walking beat on Park Square. In 1968 Park Square was a haven for hookers, pimps, truckie stops and cop fighters. At the time this area belonged to District #4 and the district was asking for help in cleaning it up. Naturally it now belonged to the TPF. In the Square there was a Hayes Bickford Cafeteria, a Waldorf and a Child's Restaurant. These were places where every creep in the area would hang out. I volunteered. But my partner Gerry wanted to stay in a cruiser. The TPF walked two abreast, so now I had to find a new partner.

Paul Moscone, a kid from East Boston who had been a clerk until now wanted some fresh air, so he got the job. Paul and I made some good grabs in the Square. We made arrests for handbag snatches, fights, A&Bs and prostitution. It was kind of dirty work. It was no wonder that District #4 didn't want it. I kept wondering if I was doing the right thing. Miraculously, it seems that overnight the Waldorf closed, as did Hayes-Bickford and the truckies stop. Taking the place of those joints was a new Bunny Club, the grand opening of Bachelors III and The Great Gatsby. Overnight, Park Square with the Statler Hilton Hotel in the middle became a glamorous walking beat. Needless to say, there was a line outside the Captain's office of cops wanting to walk Park Square. What a great place to work, especially Bachelor's III where all the sports figures would go. The principle owners were Jimmy Colclough the former great receiver for the Boston Patriots and of course the one and only Joe Nameth. Athletes from every sport would eventually be there, especially Derek Sanderson who may have had a small piece of the action. Derek and I became the best of friends. Derek had such a great personality, he would talk to anyone. Derek would always ask me "Is it okay to talk to him?" And every time I would ask him for an autograph for some kid, he'd always oblige and would always show up when the Patrolman's Association was doing some thing special for the kids. Derek was the best.

I held that post for a few years until things started to change for the TPF. New captain, new sergeants, etc. Then it happened. The Deer Island House of Correction inmates were acting up. Their personnel took care of the situation but they asked for our assistance to put them to bed. On the TPF bus we went. On the way down, our new Commander Captain Moe Allen, asked the troops not to wear their side arms into the prison. Well some did and some did not think it was the right thing to do. This led to my transfer.

Ok, so here I was with a new station, a new captain, and a new partner, seemingly away from all the turmoil I had been used to. I had gone from the TPF to the District Attorney's Office Homicide to what they called the "Brighton Police." This district was considered to be a country club compared to where I was previously assigned. Brighton had a population of about eighty-five thousand people comprised mostly of college students. Brighton was bordered by Boston College and Boston University, so the biggest problems came from student drinking. The students who didn't live on campus had apartments in the hundreds of brick four-story buildings within a mile of their schools. Therefore, parking was also a major problem. It was not unusual to see The Boston Fire Department's District Chief patrolling the area along with our patrol cars. It was a major priority that these streets remained open in case of fire. So dealing with the illegal parking was always a problem.

Badge #1 – Memoirs of a Boston Cop

Now, here I was after ten years with the department. They had decided to deprogram me, giving me a break. This was not to be. I was with my new partner "Mikey" Flemmi, a cop with a great record who had been through all the riots. He was a cop with some great arrests and was popular with all the guys. Mikey was also from Roxbury having grown up about two miles from me. Although we lived close together, we "hung" on different corners. Mike had a stigma attached to him from his first day on the job.

Mikey was the kid brother of two of Boston's most ferocious killers. His oldest brother Vincent "The Animal" Flemmi was an enforcer for the Bennett Brothers in Roxbury. He was a loud, intimidating sort whose mere presence made you shutter. The law finally caught up with the "Animal" and he was sent to Walpole State Prison where one of his rivals stabbed him to death. His demise was inevitable. On the other side was his younger brother, Steven "The Rifleman" Flemmi, a hero of the Korean War. Stevie, a paratrooper, made jumps behind enemy lines in Korea and as a sniper eliminated many of the enemy brass. Stevie was a handsome, quiet guy always with a smile who could "make" any girl. He was so ruthless he could and did kill them later. Stevie's reputation was, "Don't get him angry with you or it would be goodbye."

Badge #1 – Memoirs of a Boston Cop

He was so good at his trade the big bad guys loved him. What made him so dangerous was that he could turn on you so quickly, as was the case with the Bennett Brothers who gave Stevie his first break and then he eliminated all three of them.

Again, remember that was then and this is now. Mikey Flemmi didn't have a chance. He wanted no part of what his brothers were doing but they were his brothers. Mike knew that I had been part of the Task Force, yet he never once asked me how things were going up there. The night the third Bennett brother got killed is a night to remember. It was a cold snowy night. His body was thrown into a snow bank on Harvard Street near Blue Hill Avenue in the Dorchester area. When the local sector car received the call and officers turned the body over without recognizing him, they observed what appeared to be a thirty-eight caliber pistol similar to what our detectives carry. I was working a cruiser that night and because the guys in the sector knew I was familiar with the gangland killings, they called me to see if I knew the victim. Their main concern was to make sure the victim was not a police detective. Their concern stemmed mainly from the way he was carrying his gun. With the aid of Officers John Lyndstone and Marty Coleman we identified the victim as William Bennett, the third of the

Badge #1 – Memoirs of a Boston Cop

Bennett brothers. For years no one knew who killed the Bennett's. And I remember the families begging for help from the locals as to who killed their loved ones. The law always suspected Stevie, but how could he do that? Stevie supposedly loved the Bennetts. That was then this is now.

It was 1973 and Mike and I were partners in a sector car. Mike was a great wheelman and he never would let me drive. I remember chasing stolen cars down the narrow streets of Brighton, in the Allston area, never getting into an accident and always getting our man. Mikey was, and still is, one of my best friends. Mike was not so big but he never backed down from trouble. He also was a good man to back you up. Never once do I recall having any conversations about his brothers even though he knew that I knew they were as bad as one could imagine.

One night Mike and I were in the 14-1 on patrol with Mike driving, of course, when we receive a radio dispatch for "shots fired" in the vicinity of Saint Columbkille's Church. Mike pulled up to the scene within a few minutes and after a quick search of the area Mikey cleared the call. A short time later, the dispatcher called and stated that the nuns in the convent were concerned and could we return and investigate further. We went back to the area and there on the sidewalk on Sparhawk Street, opposite Saint Columbkille's Church, was a car riddled with bullets apparently from a machine gun. Upon opening the driver's side door, I could see the driver bleeding profusely, obviously dead. He was a local bartender by the name of Michael Milano. With him and seriously wounded was a white male, identified as one Louis LaPiana. Screaming in the back seat was an unidentified white female who had also been shot, but it was not a life threatening wound. I can remember writing out the report with Mikey, never thinking this had anything to do with the "Winter Hill Gang" or any one else that I knew. None of the victims had police records so it was assumed that it was a case of mistaken identity.

I remember Mike and me later guarding the survivor, Louis LaPiana, in the intensive care unit of Saint Elizabeth's Hospital. LaPiana was hooked up to a machine to keep him alive. I remember Mikey saying he was going to pull the plug as he couldn't concentrate on the game of gin rummy that he was playing with me. This is a joke of course! For years the case went unsolved although many had their suspicions. That was then, this is now.

Badge #1 – Memoirs of a Boston Cop

Not until Whitey Bulger's right-hand man Kevin Weeks started "ratting" everyone out and after certain "hit men" found out that Bulger and Co. were informants for the FBI, Rico and others, did Johnny Martarano turn against them and admit to the mistaken identity "hit" on Michael Milano and friends. Up to this point Johnny Martarano and Stevie Flemmi were close friends. LaPiana was paralyzed for the rest of his life and died in 2001.

1973 was coming to an end and I decided to slow down a bit. I was lucky enough to get transferred to night motorcycle duty, a great job. The hardest thing I had to do was to get the Saturday night paper for the Boss. That job didn't last long. Judge Arthur Garrity saw to that. All the motorcycles were mobilized into one unit, thus forming "MOP" Mobile Operation Patrol. Our main function was to ensure the safety and welfare of the children involved with school bussing. This was somewhat of a historical event; the rest of the country was watching to see if this could really work. It didn't. The only ones benefiting from school bussing were the bus companies. They made a lot of money, while the kids were scared to death while learning nothing. Parents mobilized local politicians and got the crowds motivated while they took out their frustrations on the police. This was not only in South Boston but in the black school districts as well. Here they were, South Boston natives yelling and cursing at the TPF and MOP as if we were responsible for forced bussing. Some in the crowd actually had police officer sons on the TPF and MOP.

The elders got the younger people riled up to the extent that it became vicious. The high school was located on a hill known as Dorchester Heights, and as winter moved in and the temperature dropped, some of the radicals saw fit to get up early in the morning to open certain hydrants thus flooding and later icing the streets to prevent us from ascending the hills leading to the school and South Boston High. Because of these tactics some of our bikes went down, causing some of officers to end up in the hospital. Many of us were pelted with rocks. This lasted for over three years. Some of our officers had heart attacks and died, while some sustained serious bike accidents as a result of these serious attacks.

The TPF and MOP spent every school day working throughout the city protecting our kids while at night we would patrol the troubled areas. If you could believe it, we were averaging over two hundred hours a month. In one month I accumulated two hundred and fifty hours overtime. During daytime bus escorts, the bikers would return to the staging area, put their rain gear on the radio receiver, their boots on the saddle bags (without taking them off) and take a quick nap. At night we patrolled Southie and Charlestown, breaking up fights and gangs of thugs throwing bricks at police vehicles, MTA busses as well as any one in a car which they thought carried blacks.

After surviving the LaGrange Street shooting and the years chasing Barboza and company, there was no way I was going to get hurt chasing kids. Oh, was I so wrong. While we patrolled the streets, we worked in squads of five men with a squad leader. One night while patrolling I remember approaching an intersection leading into Bunker Hill Street, when all of a sudden all I could remember was my motorcycle proceeding without me and me bleeding from my forehead and eye. The protestors saw fit to hang piano wire corner to corner specifically to take down our bikes. Riding behind me was Cycle Officer Frank Megnia who saw me go down. Frank held my head while flagging down a Boston Ambulance assigned to that area. The force from my hitting the wire caused my helmet visor to split, breaking the impact. The wire had caused some bleeding to my head and my eye lid was slightly torn. Thank God we had ambulances standing by. The next day our Captain, John Dow informed me that the FBI had been notified and was on the way down to interview me. They arrived, interviewed me and assured me that they would get whoever was responsible. I never heard from the FBI again. That was hard to believe.

Getting back to escorting I can remember being called into South Boston High to break up a fight between blacks and whites. Some of these classrooms were in session and it was amazing to see students with their feet up on the desks with the teacher doing nothing about it. I believe that for over three years of bussing these kids learned absolutely nothing. I remember while escorting either blacks or whites driving my bike and following all I saw was their troubled faces as they were waving at me. Those kids must have thought "What are they doing to us?"

Then there was the incident at the "Rabbit Inn," a drinking hole for the locals. Daily, busses carrying blacks away from school were pelted with rocks as they passed the Rabbit Inn. Well, they made a mistake. The TPF observed what was happening so they proceeded to do what they thought was right. Unfortunately the locals complained to the politicians and they in turn wanted action against the police. In a small way they won, but they will never forget the TPF. Bussing finally ended with no one winning but those bus companies.

Badge #1 – Memoirs of a Boston Cop

Okay so now what? The TPF, because of all the pressure put on City Hall for their aggressiveness in cleaning up bad situations, had to be disbanded. I can recall vividly these same leaders begging for our help, complaining about a steady rise on black-on-black crime and how thugs were on a rampage. A new unit was formed under the command of Lt. Bob Hayden. The Lt. picked his own men and off he went into these troubled areas while transit bus drivers were harassed by gang members. Members of Hayden's squad began boarding these busses. He would then pat them down and in many instances would stack the sidewalks with weapons. There were guns, switchblades, ammo, and in many instances automatic hand guns. This went on for a period of time and these so-called thugs knew of Lt. Bob Hayden's squad.

As time went by the more aggressive the squad became. So you guessed it, those very same leaders who wanted relief from crime in their neighborhood went screaming to City Hall that Hayden's men were too aggressive with their youth. That led to "goodbye Lt. Hayden's squad." It was so frustrating and so hypocritical. Months went by, crime went back up, and the leaders again yelled for more police presence. Now, with Hayden gone and the TPF gone who do we have if an emergency arises?

Badge #1 – Memoirs of a Boston Cop

Enter: Special Operations

Those so called community groups thought they could dictate to City Hall and get whatever they wanted and do away with anything they wanted. I'll be the first to admit that I was disappointed to see my beloved TPF and MOP (Mobile Operation Patrol) being dissolved. What I didn't know was that the planning and research department, along with the brass, was putting together plans to form "The Special Operations Patrol." This unit was to consist of members of the TPF, along with members of MOP. So now they had put together the infantry along with "hell on wheels" to form the elite of the elite.

This unit had everything, motorcycles, mounted patrol, bomb squad, all under the direction of Superintendent Robert Bradley and Deputy Superintendent Martin Mulkern. The motorcycle division's primary patrol function varied. The bikes worked in pairs, saturating the city while issuing traffic citations and backing up the district cars. In a way it reminded me of the old TPF. Here we were, again in training, working with three foot batons. But now we had brand new Harley Davidson motorcycles, new Glock semi-automatics with ultra penetrating ammunition and we trained as teams for use in SWAT situations. The purpose of the teams was to make sure that we had at least one swat team working at night.

This was a far cry from the TPF SWAT team that some thought was the first in the country. I can recall hundreds of times being activated for an entry, putting on our SWAT get-up and being loaded into the wagon with the team and not knowing where we were going. Then we'd arrive and were hurriedly advised as to what we were going after while another leader would advise us as to how to gain entry. Many times upon entry we got what we were looking for without much of an incident. But then again there were times we were met by suspects who refused to drop their weapons, but luckily my team always prevailed. There were many times our information was false but none of us ever got seriously hurt. I can remember one time while trying to gain entry to one of the apartments in the Franklin Park project, I was supposed to be the second man in with my shotgun. I tripped. Down to the ground I went while five SWAT members trample over me to gain entry. After that, I was the talk of the unit.

Later that summer Special Operations received word that the Pope was coming to Boston. I remember the thrill of being a part of that team that met the Pope at Logan Airport and then escorted him by motorcycle and being on his left side upon his descending from his Alitalia jumbo jet. I remember how he gave us all his blessing. I can recall escorting him through the Sumner Tunnel and then to Saint John's Seminary in Brighton. After a short visit he came out and we escorted him to the Cathedral of the Holy Cross for a brief stop.

Then an incident occurred that remains embedded in my memory. I pulled up from behind and to his left and came face to face with the Pope. Here we were in front of the high school from which I graduated. With that, the Pope acknowledged me and handed me a white rose. I gently kissed the rose and laid it ever so gently into my right saddlebag. From there it was off to the Boston Common and an outside mass attended by thousands. Later I thought, boy this is much better than hunting down Joe Barboza. Plus there was a big difference between looking at the "Animal" and then facing the most holy man in the world. All this and driving a Harley Davidson too!

The good times and the bad

It was so easy thinking about the good times I had on the job. It's so hard to express just how fraternal this job really is. It is so "tight" that it gets to the point where you don't want to associate with anyone other than "cops."

Badge #1 – Memoirs of a Boston Cop

And our wives have to be of a certain breed. Without a doubt, the hardest job in the world is being married to a cop. The wives virtually see their husbands overnight. In most cases from an always smiling, always happy hubby to a suspicious somewhat less sensitive guy than he once was. The parties we had, especially while on the TPF, were always so much fun that even the wives had fun. You became so much like a family that you just couldn't enjoy conversation with anyone other than cops or their wives. And what really hurt was when one of us or our family "hurt." In my thirty-nine and a half years on the job I have lost many friends who either got seriously hurt or were killed in the line of duty.

This was the case with a friend of mine, Officer Roy Sergei, who was killed chasing a felony suspect through an alley in the South End. I had to guard the "suspect" Ted Osuki, the son of an Asian millionaire, and protect him from bodily harm. How do you figure, a Marine, coming home from Vietnam in one piece, only to be killed after being struck by an Amtrak train as he searched for guns taken during a Brighton housebreak. That was the case of Officer Tommy Gill, a detective, who served "Nam" only to die in the line of duty here. Tommy was a South Boston native, handsome, always smiling, with lots of friends. I remember thinking that guys like Tommy would live forever.

"Bucky Johnson," was a traffic cop doing his thing at the corner of Tremont and Stuart Streets. Always smiling, and joking with the motorist's as they passed him, one day, he was approached by a citizen who claimed that there was a fight in the "Tam" Cafe, a joint across from his traffic post. The citizen failed to tell Bucky that one of them had a gun. Officer Johnson walked in and was shot dead. I was a young officer then and I remember what a strong impact that shooting had on me.

I can also recall all of the dangerous assignments we would get while on the TPF and how lucky we were. One officer who was not so lucky was Jerry Hurley, a foot soldier who transferred to the Bomb Squad thinking it would be less strenuous for his wife. It proved to be fatal for Jerry. He was murdered in Roslindale in October of 1991 by a bomb blast as he was investigating "suspicious persons."

One incident that is imbedded in my mind, occurred on February 19, 1993 a Friday night just before roll call. In the guard room getting ready for first-half duty at Area A-1, joking and telling stories while getting on the elevator for the ride down to the garage to begin my motorcycle patrol downtown, Officer Tommy Rose got off the elevator and said, "See ya later Frankie." I remember putting my gear into my saddlebags on my bike and was just about to start it when I heard two loud "bangs." I thought nothing of it at first, but then all hell broke loose. Tommy had been shot by a prisoner upstairs near the booking area while escorting him to make his phone call. Tommy was hurried to an ambulance, and instead of my going on patrol, I escorted Tommy to the Mass General Hospital emergency room. I stayed with Tommy as they wheeled him into the operating room, and I remember the doctors being optimistic at first. The family came in and they were in the waiting room, and the doctors told them that they were doing everything that they could do. But it was not to be. Tommy died on the operating table.

Those were only a few of the "brothers" that I knew and were very close to.

There were so many good times and luckily they outweighed the bad times. From the beginning, first escorting President Lyndon Johnson and covering and escorting Vice President Hubert Humphrey right up to the Pope and in between hundreds of high profile politicians, movie stars, and sports celebrities. Also, being in the visitor's dugout while on duty at Fenway Park, I met the manager of the Texas Rangers during their first year in the American League. It was Ted Williams, my idol. Those were some of the good times.

Then on a sadder note... Since I joined the department, seventeen of my brother officers were killed or died from injuries sustained in the line of duty.

I can recall so vividly escorting the funeral of Walter Schroeder who a few days earlier had been shot in the back and killed while responding to a bank alarm in Brighton on Western Avenue. His killer, William "Lefty" Kilday was spotted by the State Police on the Mass Turnpike and was being pursued with sirens blaring. We were on Market Street escorting Walter and listening on our "walkie-talkies" for the progress of the chase in which they were successful.

Ironically Walter's brother John, a detective in the South End was killed while investigating holdups in that area...

Reality

So what was really going on in the city of Boston during my illustrious career? Within most departments police officers graduate from their academies after a long, tedious and very stressful amount of time, sometimes as much as six months. Without a doubt police officers while in their academies receive the best training their city can give and without a doubt they are ready for just about anything. They are prepared physically and academically with the resources they currently have (computers, better weapons, communications, etc.) What they need most and what they can't learn in any police academy is "common sense."

In my rookie year of "1964," I remember hitting the street after three months in the Academy. The "common sense" came from listening to veteran officers who I rode with and keeping my mouth shut while observing and learning. It came from thinking back about how officer Carrozza complained about his being with a rookie. I remember how much I learned just from on-the-job training and listening, and I wouldn't dare complain. Always on my mind from my days in grammar school was the word "THINK." It seems that today's young officers are more interested in getting an air-conditioned cruiser and in the winter a warm and comfortable car. And if they don't get one, they walk right into the Captain's office. My how times have changed!

Badge #1 – Memoirs of a Boston Cop

Protocol is only a word now, but I can remember in my early days walking into my first assigned precinct (District 13) and then walking by the front desk and saluting even though the seat was empty. Back then if you were to see the Captain you were in serious trouble. The chain of command was always in effect. And as far as rookies listening and learning from older officers now, "Forget about it!"

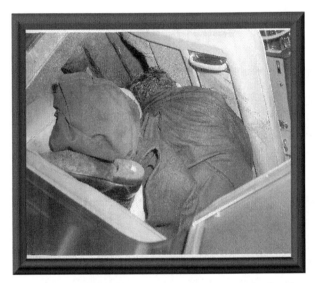

Bratsos's body on top of DePriscio's body found in the back seat of Arthur Tash Bratsos's 1965 grey Cadillac
Both men were killed at the Nite Lite Café.
Their bodies were thrown into the back of Bratsos's car which was parked in front of the alley outside the Nite Lite Café.

Badge #1 – Memoirs of a Boston Cop

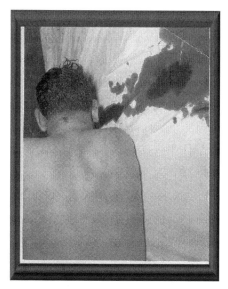

Arthur "Tash" Bratsos's body taken from
the back seat of his Cadillac

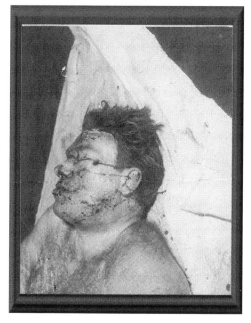

Thomas DePriscio's body after being taken out of
the back seat of the Cadillac

Badge #1 – Memoirs of a Boston Cop

*Police (Frank on left) and emergency personnel speed
fatally wounded Patrolman Thomas Rose (inset) to
Mass General Hospital for emergency surgery*

*Pope John Paul in limo
being escorted by Frank DeSario*

10

Our FBI

And now looking back and reminiscing about the old days, I can't help but think how naive I really was. Yeah I was street smart and I was a pretty tough kid and I always thought I could handle any situation. If I couldn't, I knew my "brothers would be there to help."

But what I learned was that that was only true in the uniform branch, especially with the officers of the Tactical Patrol Force and Special Operations. With the TPF, I knew that if I were ever in trouble and needed assistance, all I had to do was get to my radio to say "Officer in Trouble." And during the hundreds of times with our SWAT Team, I never had to worry about my back being covered. Working with officers you could trust helped with the success of those entries. Even when I returned to those specialized units I still had no idea of what was really going on while working with the Task Force.

After thirty-five years on the job, I finally got to learn the truth "at least some of it" from the hoodlums themselves. It goes beyond mere betrayal. The thought that other law enforcement personnel were on the side of murderers that the task force was looking for, and for the FBI along with all American boy agent John Connolly, to have a part in this, makes my blood boil and emphasizes the word " betrayal."

When I say I was naïve, I was, especially when I had to find this out thirty-five years later. All in all, in my mind I thought I was satisfied with what I had accomplished, and for the most part I thought I had put it all together. I could understand how Bulger groomed Connolly, made him what he was for his own particular purpose. It wasn't hard to believe but it made me sick when after retiring, I had to read in the newspapers how an FBI agent could be so dirty, and then have the ability to get to other FBI agents and also his superior. Although Connolly was making big bucks (so many that he wasn't even cashing his paychecks) and living a luxurious life, no one had ever heard of him.

What further infuriated me was when the story broke and Connolly denied everything. I was infuriated how he said he was only doing his job. All hell broke loose when the squeeze was put on some of Bulger's bag men, fearing that they would do time and they started making deals. They told of the whereabouts of bodies that were buried in the greater Boston area, and with the help of Bulger's number one man Kevin Weeks, described how they were killed by Bulger and Flemmi while being protected by Agent Connolly. Sadly any one that dared go to the FBI with any information was intercepted by Connolly and that person would end up dead. Meanwhile, Connolly, with the help of Flemmi, was walking the streets of the North End especially Prince Street where Gerry Angiullo's offices were. Along the way with some technicians they were able to bug Angiullo's offices along with other property on Prince Street. Connolly couldn't lose while walking the North End. He had Flemmi with him, an Italian who Angiullo tried to recruit. The furthest thing from anyone's mind was the possibility that Flemmi was a "rat." Well it turned out he was, big time. Connolly succeeded and with the help of his friend "Flemmi" took down the local mafia Boss and his brothers.

Let's try to put this together. It was the early 60's. How does the Task Force stop the murders? How do we find out who the good guys are and who the bad guys are on the sixth floor of the DA's office? How do we find out how or who the intelligence detective worked for? And most important, who was Commander John Doyle of the Domestic Affairs Unit? What we do know about him was that as a patrolman, he directed traffic at the corner of Beacon and Charles Streets at the foot of the courthouse. It appeared that every morning the DA's car with Mr. Garrett Byrne inside would pass

Officer John Doyle and as a result they became friends. Before you knew it John Doyle was assigned to the DA's office of Domestic Affairs with the brand new title of "Commander." This man was put in charge of the men we were told not to talk to. Now the Commander, a man who never took a promotional exam in his career, all of a sudden became a Superintendent from his civil service rank of patrolman.

What baffled us most was how they could be at the scene of a murder before us even though we would get the call. Did Lt. Ingenere know something and not tell us? Was it only our imaginations? Why did he not want us to talk to them? There were times when both Doyle and Ingenere would meet at a scene and immediately the two would start arguing. Every time Old Sal would reassure Doyle that he was only a patrolman. That infuriated Doyle. Now looking back, could H Paul Rico have had a contact in the DA's office? Would Barboza hate enough to dare to put a contract on us?

Was it our imagination or was it real the night we were having dinner as "The Task Force" at Arty's Fireside Restaurant in Dedham, when all of a sudden the Lieutenant received a phone call and upon his return to our table he yelled "Let's go back into Boston,"

Badge #1 – Memoirs of a Boston Cop

without Sal telling us what was going on?

All those nights we were riding, searching, all of the North Shore from Lynn and once all the way down to Cape Cod on a tip that a body was buried there and then coming up with nothing. There were the phone calls we received in the daytime regarding the whereabouts of friends of Barboza which turned out to be fruitless. One of Barboza's and D'Amico's (before he was murdered) favorite hangouts was the Beach Ball Bar on the strip along Revere Beach, a joint where just about all the hoods and wanna-be hoods "hung out" Lt. Ingenere always made it a point for us to drop in especially on weekends. This was Barboza's favorite joint.

Along with the "Animal" and "Chico" there would be Guy Frizzi, Nicky Femmia, and occasionally Arthur "Tash" Bratsos, whose idol was Joe Barboza. Now this group ruled the Beach Ball. This group along with a bunch of small time hoods instilled fear in the owners while they let them run the place. For some strange reason the place attracted a lot of beautiful girls. I remembered the name "Beach Ball" because of the story I had heard of how a few years back, Detective McCain, before coming to the Task Force, and at the time he was assigned to MDC headquarters, had a confrontation with Joe "the Animal." It seemed that Detective Joe was attempting to bring Barboza in. Barboza threatened Detective Joe stating he was brave because he had a badge and a gun. With that McCain invited "The Animal" down to the Revere Beach Boardwalk. It seemed that old Detective Joe did some fighting himself while in the U.S. Navy and did some boxing as a heavyweight.

They went 'at it' near the boardwalk with Detective Joe coming out on top. Barboza hated McCain. And imagine his reaction finding out later that McCain was now a member of the Task Force. This infuriated him more. He always thought it was like some kind of vendetta against him. Detective McCain had so much disdain for Barboza as did Barboza for Joe. While on the Task Force, one night in Revere Beach they casually bumped into each other. As "The Animal" threw a punch, McCain threw one loud punch knocking Barboza on the beach. Heated words were delivered as "The Animal" walked away. Detective Joe wanted "The Animal" badly, and McCain was afraid of no one.

One night at the Beach Ball there was this kid from Dorchester, hitting and doing well with the girls in the club. His name was Arthur Pearson, a tall maybe

Badge #1 – Memoirs of a Boston Cop

6'4" two hundred pound Adonis dancing and having a ball with "The Animal" and Chico's girls. Apparently Arthur was a very naive person playing outside of his Fields Corner Backyard, and coming to Revere because he knew the women were aplenty. Arthur was making his moves when at the same moment Chico and the "Animal" were making theirs. They moved in on Arthur and had words. Then instantly Pearson was cut from his belly button-down to his crotch and was bleeding profusely. The kid from Dorchester almost died that night. But because he was so strong and healthy up until that point he survived, just barely. During his stay at a Boston Hospital friends and family came to visit Arthur and I'm sure they told him what a mistake he had made. I remember walking into his hospital room along with Lt. Ingenere and observing him lying there in bed, tubes running out of his nose, wires coming out of his genital area, an intravenous in his left arm, and bandages covering his nose and cheekbones. I remember standing at the foot of the bed, listening and watching as Lt. Ingenere interviewed him. It seemed that he had gotten the message and refused to talk even though Lt. Sal threatened him for being a hostile witness.

There was no doubt about it. It was the "carvemanship" of Chico and the brawn of Barboza that did in Pearson. He did keep his mouth shut and was never heard from after that.

We were still searching and hoping and still getting phone calls and "tips" as to what Barboza might be planning. Up to this point none of us would dare to admit, or were crazy enough to think that Bulger along with Flemmi with the help of H Paul Rico could lure Barboza away from being a hit man for Angiullo and Co. What a dream team, Bulger, Flemmi and Barboza. Meanwhile, one of their closest associates, Johnny Martaranno, not yet knowing that his partners were "rats," kept doing his thing at the behest of Bulger and Flemmi. Things were going so smoothly for them that they could do anything they wanted. They could murder, push drugs to the kids in their own neighborhood and Flemmi, and double cross his best friend and Mafia Boss, Frank Salemmi.

Even as I reminisce about my entire career, no matter where I go it all comes back to the DA's office. When I left the Task Force I thought I was finally rid of the Gangland adventure. Upon leaving I was involved in so many things related to the DA's office. When Barboza was spilling his guts out up at Suffolk Superior Court, there I was my SWAT Team outside the courtroom door protecting him while he was lying his guts out and sending innocent men to jail. Of course no one knew it at the time. I didn't know it so let me repeat myself. I thought we were getting something. At the time the names he was giving up meant nothing to me, so I assumed at the time that they were indeed murderers or co-conspirators so I didn't much care. But I found out it was kind of ironic that after chasing the "Animal" here I was protecting him.

As I was sitting in the lobby of the court I just reminisced and remembered how confused I always was. I recall sitting there and thinking how honored I was at the time to be a part of that unit, and then one incident I recalled which at the time I thought nothing about...

One of the Task force's first assignments I remember was receiving a call regarding a cache of guns and ammo along with dynamite being buried in the yard of a bar and grill on Bennington Street in East Boston, a place where Barboza and company often frequented. We got the call at the DA's office and we immediately bolted to East Boston Court, obtained a warrant and proceeded to the bar and grill. At the time I remember thinking nothing of it as we arrived at the scene, only to find that at the other side of the hall was Commander John Doyle. The Bomb Squad was digging up the back yard and Doyle's men were thoroughly searching the premises, while I ("fresh paint") was being pushed aside like a pinball machine. While I was bumping into detectives, and trying to stay out of the way, I observed a refrigerator and decided to open it and find something to drink. Lo and behold, in the freezer, behind the ice cube trays were several loaded clips of M-1 ammo.

Here I was, in the corridor of Suffolk Superior Court babysitting Barboza, while thinking back to all those nights and days trying desperately to get him off the street. I remember while I was inside Giambi's Grill that night in East Boston, trying to stay out of the way, and then opening up the refrigerator. The detectives along with the bomb squad were digging up the yard next to the Grill. I remember that they found no dynamite, but did come up with a (as they put it) small but deadly arsenal of guns and ammunition. The dynamite, detectives were led to believe, was acquired for use in a future gangland murder in revenge for the slayings of Arthur "Tash" Bratsos of Medford and Thomas J DePriscio Jr. of Roslindale.

After I found the Ammo in the freezer, I remember being pushed aside by the "Commanders" men where they proceeded to completely search the freezer and then found more ammunition for small arms along with a shotgun and shells and a 38 caliber revolver, a Lugar, and a 32 caliber automatic, all loaded. These, three other detectives found, behind a loose ceiling panel in a rest room between the bar and kitchen. In the cellar they found a club, a baseball bat, a blackjack, and a bayonet, and in a box, under the counter at the front end of the bar were more small arms slugs including 38 caliber dumdums, some steel-jacketed bullets and several 30 caliber armor piercing rifle shells.

I remember the detectives talking to the owner, Louis D'Amico of East Boston, and saying that he knew nothing about the weapons or bullets that were found there. He said that the five-room apartment over the bar had been rented some time ago by Nicholas Femia but was never occupied by him and he never paid any rent for it. The reason was that Femia for the past several weeks was in the Charles Street jail on a gun carrying charge. It was later determined that Femia had worked there occasionally as a bartender with his buddy Chico D'Amico who earlier in the week was murdered. All the ammunition and weapons were taken to Boston Police Headquarters and examined by our technicians. During their investigation they determined that the type of gun used to kill D'Amico was a 32 caliber carbine sold by a Florida manufacturer.

I remember it was shortly after noon when we arrived at that scene. We were met by "Commander" Doyle's men along with the Commander of District seven, Captain Francis Quinn. All of those men mentioned at Giambi's we knew were friends of Joe Barboza and were very capable of doing anything including murder. So it was thought we may have prevented a mini war. Back then no one thought of how Commander Doyle got that information and why he was there. Remember he was not assigned to Homicide. Nobody thought about it except Lieutenant Sal Ingenere. I remember him asking, with a smile on his face, "Who told Doyle's men..?" Oh, the ribbing I took the next day. There in the newspapers was a picture of me holding the clips and the caption reading "detective finds ammo belonging to gangland figures."

During the testimony given by Barboza, everything seemed to be elementary. He was on the stand, giving testimony, getting even with a lot of his ex-associates in the North End, especially the Angiullos while knowing there was a $50,000 tag on his head and knowing he was going to avenge "Chico's" murder while knowing that Angiullo and Co. were responsible. He was sending innocent men to prison for life while secretly he was in alliance with Bulger and Flemmi and FBI agent H Paul Rico. And he knew that he was going to walk out of that court room soon and be relocated to another state under an assumed name. Local law didn't care much as they assumed that what Barboza testified to was the truth. So the city was getting rid of the North End murderers as well as the "Animal."

Out of the court now, I was back on the street and into the North End. I became somewhat educated in the DA's office mainly because of the tools we had to work with and from the fear we instilled in some of our "clients." Again I must reiterate that I found out the truth, or at least most of it, on the street in the North End, and yes in the newspapers over thirty years later.

My last ten years on the job patrolling the North End turned out to be the best of my career. I did have an edge in gaining their confidence by being one hundred percent Italian and having them know that I demanded respect. I found that the residents there spoke their mind, say it like it is and love the better things in life. Like most neighborhoods, the theme was "treat them right and they will treat you right." And so as time went by I had numerous friends. One thing I always knew was that if I were ever in trouble on the street I would have plenty of help as I think about that incident on Prince Street thirty-five years earlier.

One of the things I enjoyed most in the North End was receiving disturbance calls regarding incidents on neighborhood corners or at playgrounds where the local kids had the reputation of being very boisterous "loud-mouths." They have their own style and they often reminded me of myself growing up in Roxbury. Now believe me we had our problems there. Like most neighborhoods the North End had its share of troublemakers and druggies. But we knew who they were and I like to think I spoke their language and they knew I was there to help if they wanted.

Frank DeSario on the left
holding an M-1 30 caliber ammo clip
which he found in the freezer.
Next to Frank is a detective from John Doyle's office.

11
Well, All of a Sudden

The North End spoke its own language. Amazingly, they could have a complete conversation without saying a word and had a knack for taking care of business on their own. Traditionally, they didn't trust too many people. But once that trust was established, they "accepted" you as one of their own. Before establishing this trust, they could be the most standoffish people in the world. When they accepted you, you became like a part of their family; they had their own code of ethics.

I found that when they offered you food and you refused, they took it very personally. The easiest way to get along with them was to sit down and "mangia" eat. The North End had its own agenda too. They knew what the score always was. They did what they had to do. If it was not the right thing, and they got caught, it was their own fault. For the most part, they knew right from wrong. The "bad guys" generally knew how to play Cops and Robbers, so it was always understood – "mess up, get caught, you're gone."

I can remember like it was yesterday, how certain restaurants in the Hanover Street area were the favorites of both the cop brass and the local "La Cosa Nostra." Giro's on Hanover Street at Commercial, a half block from the "Nite Lite Café" was a favorite of many law enforcement officers as well as being a mini headquarters for "wise guys" and yet no one did anything there but eat.

Al's on Hanover Street was the "Blue Front," a favorite to all. I can remember DA Garrett Byrne asking me to drive him there and as I was driving I thought "Oh my God, I know this is a bookie joint." We walked in, everyone acknowledged him, saying hello Mr. Byrne while two games of Gin Rummy continued to be played while all "other action" stopped at least for the moment. We had a meal that I will never, never, never forget. The food was just delicious. Served there were dishes only your mother would have prepared. It was like someone calling "Time Out" while we ate. And then one day we saw construction going on there and then a condominium was built and we were heartbroken.

Biking down North Street, I was passing the old TPF headquarters in the old District one building. I stopped, looked up and recalled one very eerie roll call we had a few years back. Imagine if you can the TPF standing at roll call in formation, at attention, waiting for their assignment. Standing there was Officers Mike

Flemmi, brother of the notorious "rifleman." Next to him was Officer Randy La Matinna, son of the notorious "Ralphy Chong" La Matinna, and behind them Officer Gary Bratsos, whose brother was murdered by Randy's father.

Imagine when all of a sudden Officer La Matinna yells out to Bratsos to "Stop Staring" or else do something. All the TPF men knew the connection but were unsure of what roll Stevie had played. Try to figure it out. First we have Stevie Flemmi walking the North End with agent H Paul Rico trying to infiltrate the headquarters of "The Angiullo's" and Chong being a strong Mafia Ally. Then how did Officer Bratsos feel, knowing that Officer Randy's father killed his brother? If that is not confusing I don't know what is. The irony of all this is, and I would bet money on it, that these three cops were dedicated police officers with great records and yes, all three are great friends of mine. Maybe it was just as confusing to them as it was to me. I'm willing to bet that Mikey knew nothing of the details of the relationship that his brother had with "Whitey" Bulger or the relationship with H Paul Rico and later with Agent John Connolly and a couple of other scumbags with the FBI.

Thinking back, with what I now know, I can remember getting on my bike and going way out to any one of the wharfs and shutting the bike down, looking out into the ocean, watching the planes land and take off at Logan Airport and thinking "Am I imagining, or did this really happen?"

We had Barboza finishing up his testimony at Suffolk Superior Court. I remember every floor of the court house had at least one squad of police officers on it, and outside it was surrounded by SWAT Teams. We had to call for some outside help, just in case. Only Joe Barboza knew the truth. We certainly knew he had enemies right down the street less than a mile away in the North End and his friends in Revere and East Boston were either in the can or hiding. We didn't know for sure what his affiliation with Flemmi and Bulger was. So it was out of the courthouse, down the stairs and into the "Tombs" where a few years earlier he had been booked and locked up for at least half a day. Now we were finally getting rid of Joe Barboza, not anywhere close to the way we wanted to end our relationship but at least he was going to be out of Boston.

The Boston papers were covering the event as if it was the "World Series." Rumors around Boston Police Headquarters were that a top lieutenant in the local Mafia by the name of Joseph Russo had the contract on the "Animal." Now he belonged to the Feds. Now it was their responsibility to relocate him and let him live under an assumed name, which he did. During his stay in New England, he was known to have killed at least forty people and he enjoyed the notoriety. I mean this guy was so bad that he once killed a man who had witnessed him killing a guy by the name of Romeo Martin. The poor guy worked for a soft drink company and he was loading a machine when he witnessed Joe in action.

Joe looked up and saw the witness, walked over to him and while the man begged for his life he shot him dead. There was a time when we had a friend of Joe's in for questioning on an unrelated matter. He stated to us that the "Animal" once told him that when he "clipped" someone "it was like fucking Marilyn Monroe." That's how much he enjoyed killing people.

Okay so now he's out of Boston, and believe me a lot of people sighed with relief. Joe "The Animal" we later found out went to the West Coast and continued in his murderous ways at least two more times in the San Francisco area. It appeared that Joe must have felt invincible since he began to let his guard down a wee bit. Joe Barboza finally got what he deserved. One beautiful day as he was getting out of a vehicle he took a blast from a shotgun ending his life. Word has it that Joe Russo took a trip to the West Coast. This was the end of Joseph Barboza! Word got out quickly in Boston, and man the celebrations began. I remember how we celebrated that night. He was no loss to the community.

Here we were in the mid nineties and I was closing in on sixty years of age. Impossible! And I was closing in on thirty years of motorcycle duty. I never thought of my age much, but as time went by I couldn't help hearing "Hey old timer how ya doin?" Walking in and out of the station house I would hear (in a joking manner) "hey, when you gonna quit and give a young kid a break?" At first it didn't bother me but eventually I began to realize that I should begin thinking of "retiring" or at least slowing down a whole lot.

Here I was, senior motorcycle officer in the city. Then I was thinking of the beginning of my career. I went from The Tactical Patrol Force to the District Attorney's office "Task Force," on to the Mobile Operations Squad and then on to Special Operations, and a member of the elite SWAT Team for twenty years. So maybe I should begin to think that I may be pushing my luck. What I did, was promise myself that I would relax, stay out of trouble and slow down for a couple of years.

During the last five years of my career, the Captain, Captain Bernard "Bernie" O'Rourke, (a sharp level headed boss) and a city boy, assigned me to the Downtown Crossing for the purpose of being highly visible and to prevent holdups in the downtown area. I would stay there until maybe seven-thirty and then head down to the North End. I was to keep Hanover Street clear and to patrol the small streets and alleys while backing up the sector car. Not a bad assignment! At the downtown crossing I would park my bike and make myself visible. I would just sit there watching the shoppers walk by. Sitting there between Filene's and Macy's department stores I was making friends and talking to the merchants and fielding their complaints. Occasionally a cruiser would drive by, stop and the officer would ask, "Frankie, who do you know to get an assignment like that?" At seven-thirty I would go down to the North End and straight to Modern Pastry for a great cup of coffee and an occasional cannoli. I would sit there with the owner "Giovanni" and his wife "Pina" and just talk and enjoy each other's company, while greeting the customers as they just kept filing in. At least three times a week Marie Salvati along with her girl friend Marie would come in and join us. Inevitably the conversation would turn to her husband "Joe the

Horse" and how was he doing. She would always say Joe was doing fine. She would always talk about the people who believed in Joe and would always say, "How can I ever repay them?" and eventually "You guessed it" the name Joe Barboza would come up with great disdain on Marie's face. Deep down inside it was obvious Marie was a hurt woman.

At about eight-thirty or so I would sit on my bike watching the traffic go by and say "Hi" to all residents of the North End. Almost nightly Joe "the horse" would come out of his favorite restaurant "Bricco's" to say hi. Joe always talked like one of the boy's but when the conversation turned to his wife and kids or grandkids tears would always fill his eyes.

I always wondered how Joe could look at my uniform and at what I represent. This was only my imagination. When we finished talking we would always hug each other, and he would always say "be careful Frankie." Now Joe was just past seventy, so he grew up in the "old school." Like I said before, Joe was no Angel growing up during some tough times, but Joe was not what Barboza claimed him to be.

I had so many friends in that area that it was hard to keep moving. When the weather turned bad and cold, the merchants would yell for me to come inside and get warm. Such would be the case with my good friend George D'Amilio, owner of a restaurant called "No.5 North Square." I had known George and his wife Lillian since the mid sixties beginning with my time in the DA's office. George had an uncle Fiore who was murdered in a parking lot as he was walking to his car less than four blocks from his home. I can see George's grandfather's face with tears pouring down begging for us to find his son's killer. It was pretty well known, and George knew it, that Fiore was doing the wrong thing and he was warned about it, but Fiore was stubborn.

Lillian, George's wife had a brother named Al Orlandino who was a Boston Police Officer and occasionally rode the bike with me. George had another brother, Christy who was a cook and a heavy gambler, and was unable to work for a living. He had a thing for the horses, not betting on them, but trying to fix them. Christy was a good kid but he was a "wanna-be." Christy took one in the head also adding more hurt to the family. George was left with the property and he proceeded to start a successful restaurant business. We were and still are good friends. In the cold of the winter, that would be my "dugout" while nothing was going on in the street.

Badge #1 – Memoirs of a Boston Cop

When nothing was going on in the street, into five North Square I would go. I would sit with George, while some of our friends would come in. Tony DeMarco, the former welter weight champ of the world would sit at our table along with one of his handlers and long time friend "Fernando" who was a buyer of sea food, especially lobster and crabs. From time to time George would throw a bunch of lobsters and crabs in the pot. While we waited we sat and played all sorts of trivia, from sports to Godfather trivia. As a matter of fact our table was nicknamed "the Goodfellas" table.

My tour of duty was always almost up, but I would always stay long after my tour was over. Our table was next to the rest rooms, and I remember how the customers would look at us as we sucked on lobsters and crabs. They must have thought we were cannibals. In the trivia game it was amazing to see just how knowledgeable Tony was in sports. Tony could remember fighters names from the time of John L. Sullivan to the present and Tony would tell the story of how he got discovered.

As a kid growing up on Fleet Street, he would forever be getting into fights with sailors. Although he was only fifteen or sixteen years old, he would knock them out and then run home. His mother would greet him at the door and send him to his room. Tony was so good at fighting that his friends encouraged him to box for a living, but he was too young. Fernando, his close buddy, and the rest of his friends decided that Leonard Liotta, his real name, along with the real Tony DeMarco and his birth certificate should visit Father Mario up at Sacred Heart Church where they could make Lenny, legally Tony DeMarco.

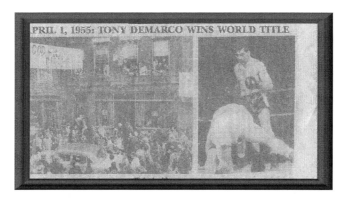

Tony *DeMarco winning title at Boston Garden*

12

End of the Ride

One of the most incredible things I think of now is how the make-up of the department has changed. In March of 1964 my academy class consisted of forty-four Boston Police recruits and five recruits from the Brookline Police Department. They were all white males with the exception of one of Boston's Finest. His name was Paul, and I can remember the "friendly" abuse he would take. We kept asking him where he was from, and he would say from Boston and that he was half Spanish. We all knew he was uncomfortable at first, but as time went by the class became very tight.

As time goes by into your career, occasionally one would bump into a classmate and the closeness you would feel toward each other was remarkable. We could relate to all the uncomfortable assignments we got at the academy. We could recall all the good times and the bad times while always keeping tabs on each other's progress in the department. Conversations among brother officers would always include how many "Bosses" came out of their class, and others would state how many weirdoes they had in theirs. The camaraderie among classmates for the most part was intense. Everyone would watch the progress of each other's career, and would ask "How's he doing?"

Comparing the make-up of the recruits of the sixties to that of the present time is mind boggling. In order to serve and communicate with such a diverse population, departments must, and do hire many minority personnel in order to better serve the entire community. Now, when these recruits begin, they not only learn the basics as we did but now they learn all about "Community Policing" and everything they do will include the operating of computers. Not only are the classes very diverse they are much larger, sometimes over one hundred in a class. And they are in the academy for over six months. So when an officer closes in or is nearing retirement he knows he is not programmed for all this new technology, and it is time to go. The rules are different now and if you don't leave or "retire" you're in for trouble. Veterans are just not programmed for all this, and so you do know when to leave.

Well, here I am, thirty-nine and a half years later thinking back to that cold March day in 1964 and how thrilled and proud I was to be joining the best Police department in the country, (which I truly believe to this day), and also thinking of all my brother and sister officers I had met and worked with through the years. The courage and bravery I had observed through the years I will never forget. Perhaps that is why I wanted to try to relate in some way just how frustrated and disappointed I am after working all those years with all those dedicated officers, only to find out the truth by reading about what really happened in the early 60's.

To sum it all up, I guess back then I could never envision any law enforcement officer, especially the FBI, protecting murderers while possibly putting other officers lives at risk, along with witnesses and other informants, as was the case with FBI agent H Paul Rico and later in the late 70's and early 80's with the likes of Agent John Connolly. Flemmi had Rico and Bulger groomed and had Connolly. And after Rico left Boston, Connolly had them both.

In the days of the Task Force I can remember seeing law enforcement personnel from every state agency, including the FBI walking the corridors of the courthouse. Those people worked for Commander John Doyle. We in Lieutenant Ingenere's squad had only Boston officers and two Metropolitan Detectives. I never saw Rico nor do I know if he was ever in or around the "Commander's" office, but now thinking back to the first week on the Task Force, I remember being ordered to pick up a mob associate by the name of Brian Halloran and I thought nothing of it. I remember him co-operating with us and he left a free man. Brian didn't last long; he was gunned down in a car leaving a restaurant sometime later. "Coincidence," I don't know.

Okay, finally I did what I wanted to do. Was this all my imagination? I don't know. What I do know is that my career was one hell of a ride and I wouldn't change cars for anything.

Now all I had to do is stay out of trouble, remain a high profile and be nice to the citizens while being available to the owners and operators of the businesses in the Downtown Crossing and the North End.

After some time, the Downtown Crossing area became more and more difficult, as gang members along with "Junkies" from the outskirts of the city began pushing their wares. Complaints started coming in from merchants in the area along with department stores like Macy's and Filene's. More and more potential customers were feeling "unsafe" in the area while many of them started going to the "malls" to do their shopping. Certain groups were eyeing their prey, especially elderly women many of whom had their handbags either snatched or stolen from customer service counters while shopping. It seemed that the world was changing right in front of me and I couldn't do anything about it. It seemed the more aggressive I would get the more complaints the bosses would get, most saying I was harassing the young citizenry.

I thought I had seen it all with nearly forty years on the job. I could stake my life there was nothing I hadn't seen. Sitting on my bike one afternoon between Macy's and Filene's, about a week before my retirement, I remember being confronted by a hysterical young woman who stated that a priest was being pistol whipped by a man in front of Saint Anthony's Shrine on Arch Street right around the corner from where I was. Through the years I have become accustomed, as has any other officer with any number of years on the job, to calls similar to this. But, I thought, don't let anything bad happen now with such a short time to go. "I'm not even supposed to be here doing this."

Well, the program kicked in and around the corner I went. Before nearing the location, I remember calling the dispatcher to alert him as to what I had. I asked for a backup and requested that no sirens be used by cruisers responding to my call. As I approached the location, people were running toward me and yelling that sure enough there was a man with a gun beating a priest. There stood the man, his left hand holding the priest by the throat and in plain view I could see a gun in his right hand. With my weapon in my hand I approached the man while telling him to drop his gun. With this he turned in my direction, gun still in hand, while I was taking aim at him. Then my backup arrived unknown and unheard by the suspect and they proceeded to disarm him and in the process arrested him.

Later, I thought what a horrible way to leave the job, if I had to use my service weapon. After arresting the suspect and taking him to the station house, upon investigation it was determined that the man was a street person, high on drugs and desperately wanting money to buy more. And yes his gun was loaded. The result was fine. The arrest was given to the young backup officers who were thrilled to get it. Years ago, that would be my "pinch," but the thought of booking him, and the report by means of a computer turned me off.

Off to the North End I went and into my friend's restaurant "No. 5 North Square" where I met Tony DeMarco sitting with the owner George D'Amelio. After telling them what had just happened, George looked at me and said "Are you crazy?" Tony turned and asked, "Why don't you go home and write a book like I'm doing?"

Badge #1 – Memoirs of a Boston Cop

After sitting and talking with Tony and George about the world changing and how we were going to find solutions as to why, Tony said he was going to put it all together and write a book about his career and that my occupation wasn't the only one that had vicious and evil people in it. Now sitting back after thirty-nine and a half years, I thank God I made it and am proud of what I've accomplished.

I know that there have been many books written, detailing the events of the 1960s, and most are generally true. What I had experienced was a career full of excitement, fun, and the unknown. These were all things I could handle, things that I expected. All those years on the street I was the boss, in command, and knew the change of command. I had no suspicion at all regarding the men I worked with in my assigned units, TPF, Special Operations and District A-1. Toward the end, when I was saying goodbye to all my friends, I was having small goodbye parties along the way. It ended with a great surprise party at City Hall Plaza thrown by the Mayor, Police Commissioner Paul Evans and was co-coordinated by Special Events director Patti Pappa with my family surprisingly there. There were hundreds of officers, superintendents, motorcycle officers and even police cadets. At that time I was wearing Badge#1 for being the most senior officer in the department, so when I left, I felt fulfilled in what I had accomplished.

It was not until a few months had passed that the newspapers were breaking stories of corruption. There was FBI corruption, a few dirty State cops and maybe one Boston cop who ended up in jail and a detective whom we thought was beyond reproach. So here I was on a bright sunny, summer day reading about all this dirt while I had been in the DA's office. I wonder how FBI agent "Rico" could convince his superiors to give a mad man immunity. I'm not here trying to divulge new information about the "hits." I'm here because I'm "bullshit" to find out what really was going on while I was assigned to the DA's elite TASK FORCE and how they, the FBI, apparently didn't care if another law enforcement officer got shot or killed. Not only was I "bullshit" but I began to think, "Could I be that naïve?" But after thinking back to those days no one ever thought Bulger and Flemmi would team up with FBI agent "Rico" so, I thought smarter men than I didn't know what was going on either.

In a way I started feeling sorry for myself for not being suspicious enough to ask more questions. But now, after thinking about it, I did the best I could.

Badge #1 – Memoirs of a Boston Cop

After thinking about how badly I felt, my thoughts would shift to Marie Salvati and what she went through bringing up her kids without their father who was wrongly accused and convicted of murder. What H Paul Rico did was not just protect vicious killers; he ruined innocent men and their families. And what really got to me was when after the justice department finally got wind of what was going on with Rico and they summoned him to testify before Congress, he was confronted with questions about his roll concerning Barboza testifying about Salvati and Co. He responded by saying "What do you want me to do cry over spilled milk?" What sort of man could this Rico really be?

Maybe something good may come out of all this. I'm sure every law enforcement agency, including the coveted FBI, (which by the way would never share any bit of information with the local agencies because they were always afraid of a leak – ha) could learn from past mistakes.

Back to the Goodfella's Table

As we, Tony and George and I were sitting at our "Goodfella's" table, Tony and George started yelling at me in their North End Dialect trying to convince me to 'take care of my own life and get out of this business finally' so I could live to baby-sit for my grandkids. They reminded me that I had been boasting about this to all my friends. "I want to be baby-sitting for my grandkids one of these days. Then someone reminded me of how many officers died or were killed in the last month of their careers either by gunfire or by being run over by a truck. Both of which type instances did happen. Was I pushing my luck?

Tony and George were quick to remind me of Deputy Superintendent Edward Connolly who in the twilight of his career, after 38 years on the job, was shot trying to talk a psychopath (someone he had dealt with in the past) into giving himself up after taking his family hostage. Here is that story.

On the night of July 25, 1979, I was patrolling the North End when all of a sudden a SWAT cruiser pulled up and the officer told me to get in the car. When I got settled into the back seat he told me that an officer had been shot and was in critical condition at the Faulkner Hospital. While speeding down to #3149 Washington Street in Jamaica Plain, he clued me in on what had happened.

Badge #1 – Memoirs of a Boston Cop

It seemed that a man had taken his family hostage in their own home after Boston Police had surrounded the three level home he shared with his wife, mother, and his kids. His name was David Sundstrom, a custodian who got into a heated argument with his boss while working in a Boston Municipal building. During the outburst, the boss observed a handgun on Sundstrom's waist belt. The boss backed off and proceeded to call the Boston Police. When the custodian arrived at his Washington Street residence, he went into a psychopathic rage pushing his wife down to the floor. Somehow, she managed to call the police who were already at the residence having been tipped off by his boss. He had taken his wife hostage along with his mother and four kids ranging in age from 13 years to 9 years.

It was a hot sticky night in July and police negotiators from different angles tried to convince Sundstrom to give himself up. Meanwhile Boston Police got a rundown on who he was. He was an ex con who had been "busted" many times by Deputy Superintendent Connolly or Connolly's men so Sundstrom was known to Connolly. Eddie Connolly, upon hearing what was going on by way of his police radio, sped to the scene. When he arrived at the location, he saw that the house was surrounded by members of the SWAT team and he learned that shots had been fired out from a window. Hundreds of citizens were there witnessing what was going on.

Deputy Connolly, now with over 39 years on the job (This was about my length of service as we sat at our Goodfella's table having this discussion.) told the bosses that he knows Sundstrom and he thinks he can talk him into surrendering. Connolly then went up the five stairs leading to the foyer and began calling for the suspect to give himself up. Meanwhile my SWAT team positioned ourselves in strategic spots so we could take him out if need be. I remember the first position I had was behind a car. As Connolly entered the foyer calling for Sundstrom to come talk to his "friend," a shot rang out and Connolly was down. The suspect ran back into his home and yelled out that he will never give up. Police rushed to the aid of Deputy Connolly and proceeded to take him to Faulkner Hospital where he was clinging to life after being hit with a 45-caliber slug.

This incident had begun at about 3:15p.m. and it was after 8:15p.m. when our SWAT team was about to rush the building. At that moment out came Sundstrom hiding behind his family who were being used as a shield. I thought, "what a lowly form of man.." Connolly survived by lived only a few more years and was in pain until the day he died.

Now, back at our Goodfella's table I looked at George and then at Tony and I told them, "Okay boys, let's play trivia. Enough is enough... It is time for me to stop and play with those grandkids. It is time to end my career."

Summing up all of my experiences and sharing them with so many people, I feel honored to have been a part of such a great police department.

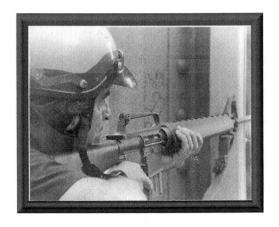

Frank with SWAT team waiting for the armed suspect David Sundstrom

A police officer and a civilian aid holding up
Deputy Superintendent Ed Connolly
after he was shot in the chest

Revving up for retirement

Frank DeSario at City Hall

Revving up for retirement

Surprise Retirement Party

for Frank DeSario at City Hall

<u>Badge #1 – Memoirs of a Boston Cop</u>

Badge #1 Boston Cop

Frank DeSario

<u>Badge #1 – Memoirs of a Boston Cop</u>

Frank DeSario is retired from the

Boston Police Department.

He lives in Dedham

Massachusetts with his wife Geri.

He treasures his Badge #1.

Dedication

I dedicate this book to my wife, Geri, who was always waiting for me, while she was raising our three kids in our little apartment, never knowing if I would be coming home. She is truly a police officer's wife.

And, to a friend I have never met but without whose help this book would not have been possible. Shelly Rosenberg, thank you.

Frank M. DeSario

58703062R00080

Made in the USA
Middletown, DE
07 August 2019